THE
Silk Ribbon
Embroidery
BIBLE

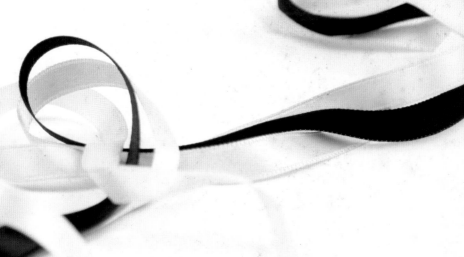

THE
Silk Ribbon
Embroidery
BIBLE

Joan Gordon

kp books
An imprint of F+W Publications, Inc.
888-457-2873

A QUARTO BOOK

First published in North America in 2005 by
KP Books
700 East State Street
Iola, WI 54990-0001

Library of Congress Catalog Card Number 2004098429

ISBN 0-89689-169-0

QUAR.SRE

Conceived, designed, and produced by
Quarto Publishing plc
The Old Brewery
6 Blundell Street
London N7 9BH

Project editor Jo Fisher
Art editor Claire van Rhyn
Designer Maggie Aldred
Illustrators John and Carol Woodcock, Carol Mula
Assistant art director Penny Cobb
Photographers Martin Norris, Paul Forrester
Copy editor Alison Howard
Proofreader Tracie Davis
Indexer Pamela Ellis

Art director Moira Clinch
Publisher Paul Carslake

Color separation by Modern Age Repro House Ltd, Hong Kong
Printed by Midas Printing International Ltd, China
10 9 8 7 6 5 4 3 2 1

Contents

Introduction

Ribbon embroidery as a creative needle art originated in France in the mid-17th century. It was used to embellish royal gowns and capes, military uniforms, waistcoats and gauntlets, and for religious vestments.

Women at the court of Napoleon II wore gowns adorned heavily with ribbons, and couture houses adopted the fashion. Wealthy women would commission dozens of gowns, because they changed clothes several times a day, beginning with a "morning coat" worn for breakfast. There was a gown for morning tea, another for luncheon, an afternoon dress for receiving guests, and a formal dinner gown. The final garment, a voluminous nightgown, would also have been embellished with ribbon embroidery. How exhausting this ritual must have been for servants!

Ribbon embroidery requires patience and practice, but most designs are worked quickly, and the results are stunning. It has been used throughout the centuries, but like most forms of embroidery its popularity goes through phases. In Victorian Britain it was used lavishly on women's hats, gowns, and accessories. In the home, it adorned cushions, linen, fire screens, and even the

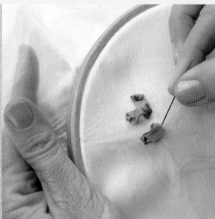

backs of hairbrushes and vanity mirrors. The technique spread throughout Europe, and to America and Canada. Many of today's designs are based on traditional and floral themes, but contemporary designers have also adopted ribbon embroidery. The results are inspiring, and it can be seen combined with beading, freestyle embroidery, charms, metallic threads, quilting, hand-dyeing, painting, ribbon burning, and appliqué. For the beginner and experienced stitcher alike, this book provides the tips and techniques required to create personalized needle art.

One of the problems ribbon enthusiasts face is the lack of information on where and how to find embroidery supplies and professional instruction. The Designers and Suppliers section provides contact details for those who have contributed to the Motif Library. Their generosity and hard work in the creation of this book will help to ensure the survival of ribbon embroidery as an embellishment technique and art form for generations to come.

Welcome to the exciting and sensuous world of ribbon embroidery. I hope that you will also discover the beauty and pleasure this luxurious needle art has to offer.

Joan Gordon

How to Use This Book

This book provides a complete introduction to ribbon embroidery, giving you the best possible start in this most exquisite of crafts.

The first chapter, Equipment and Techniques, describes all the necessary equipment and outlines the basic techniques you will need to master, from threading ribbons to caring for your finished pieces.

The Stitch Collection offers a guide to the most popular and useful ribbon embroidery stitches. Arranged into "stitch families," each stitch is described with suggestions for its use and the most appropriate ribbons to work with.

Instructions for how to work the stitch are accompanied by clear step-by-step illustrations. At the end of the chapter is an additional set of stitches, often used in freestyle embroidery, but which may also be used in ribbon embroidery designs.

The Motif Library includes over 50 beautiful designs to delight and inspire you, along with step-by-step instructions for working them. A pattern guide is included that breaks down each design into the stitches used. Symbols are used to denote each stitch, referring you back to the instructions in the Stitch Collection.

EQUIPMENT AND TECHNIQUES

Technique name with an explanation of its use.

Name of technique or piece of equipment

Equipment description

Equipment images

Tips on techniques

Step-by-step instructions show how to use the equipment or carry out the technique.

STITCH COLLECTION

Stitch family

Sample design using the stitch.

Stitch name

Stitch description

Stitch samples demonstrate the difference in appearance when the stitch is worked in different widths of ribbon.

Additional information describes how the stitch may be used.

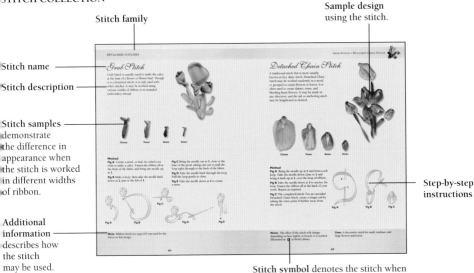

Step-by-step instructions

Stitch symbol denotes the stitch when it appears in the Motif Library.

MOTIF LIBRARY

Motif name

Motif description

Embroidered motif

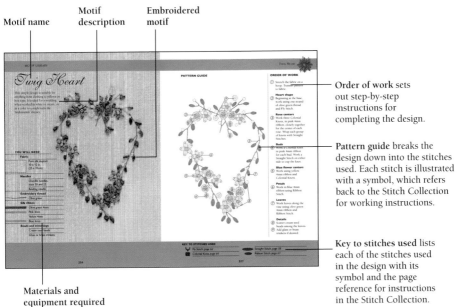

Order of work sets out step-by-step instructions for completing the design.

Pattern guide breaks the design down into the stitches used. Each stitch is illustrated with a symbol, which refers back to the Stitch Collection for working instructions.

Key to stitches used lists each of the stitches used in the design with its symbol and the page reference for instructions in the Stitch Collection.

Materials and equipment required

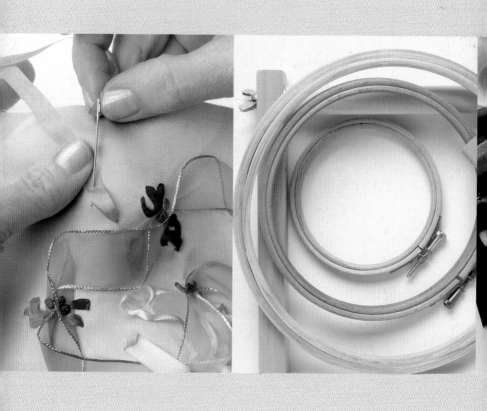

Equipment and Techniques

Working with ribbon, especially pure silk ribbon, requires specific tools and techniques. This section describes all the essential materials: the ribbons themselves, the best fabrics to use, hoops, and the various needles required. Information on the preparation and handling of ribbons and fabrics, as well as dyeing ribbon, creating backgrounds, and displaying your finished masterpiece, is also included.

Ribbons

Pure silk ribbon is expensive, but it gives the best results. It is pliable, soft, and easy to mold when cut on the bias. The widths most often used are 2mm, 4mm, 7mm, and 13mm—silk ribbons are available in metric widths only—but wider ribbon is available. Chiffon, organza, and satin ribbon may also be used.

Silk ribbon

Silk ribbon is a joy to use. It can be used to create fine, delicate detail, or dramatic floral shapes. The edges can be frayed or burned, and plain ribbons can be dyed to produce interesting effects.

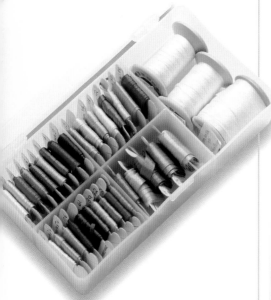

Though not specifically for ribbon, this generic craft box is extremely handy to separate the different widths of ribbon. It makes sorting through colors a breeze.

Chiffon ribbon

Chiffon ribbon made from pure silk or polyester fiber is available in a variety of widths. It molds easily into flower shapes, and may be gathered or frayed for effect. For appliqué techniques, use wire-edged chiffon ribbon.

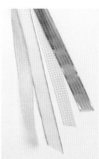

Silk organza

Silk organza is available in a variety of widths, colors, and prints, and adds texture and transparency to a design. Spark organza, as its name suggests, has an enchanting, subtle shimmer.

Satin ribbon

Satin ribbon made from pure silk or polyester fiber is available in a variety of widths. It is often used for folding techniques, in which both sides of the ribbon are visible. Narrow satin ribbon produces beautiful French Knots.

Variegated ribbon

Hand-dyed in two or more colors, variegated silk ribbons can create stunning effects. They allow you to create fabulous multihued flower petals without having to stop and re-thread your needle.

Polyester organza

This polyester/nylon blend ribbon is known for its beautiful sheen and luxurious appearance.

Wire-edged ribbon

A thin, flexible wire is woven along each edge during the manufacture. Wire-edged ribbons have many exciting possibilities. The wires can also be pulled out, allowing you to mix and match, and combine the crisp, wired ribbon with soft, fluid streamers.

Embroidery thread

Polyester and rayon are the two most popular embroidery threads. Polyester thread is made entirely from synthetic fibers that are twisted together to form thread. Part of the beauty of polyester thread is that it is resistant to discoloration caused by laundering, sun, and chemicals and has a very long shelf life. Rayon is manufactured from viscose and other natural fibers. It has much less elasticity, is weaker than polyester, is easily bleached by chemicals and the sun, and has a shelf life of only two to seven years.

Threading and Turning Ribbon

The technique of threading and turning ribbon is quite different from other embroidery techniques. You should secure the ribbon to the eye of the needle before you begin. Use short lengths of 12–13 in. (30–35cm), as the ribbon may split and fray if it is passed through the background fabric too many times.

Threading a needle

Choose a tapestry needle with an eye large enough to accommodate the width of ribbon and to make a hole large enough for the ribbon to pass through the fabric.

① To allow you to insert your ribbon easily into the eye of the needle, always begin by cutting one end of your ribbon diagonally.

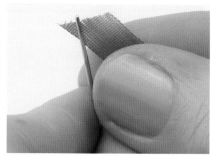

② Pass the ribbon through the eye of the needle. Insertion is easy after the ribbon has been cut on an angle.

Securing the ribbon to the eye

① Pierce the ribbon about ¼ in. (5mm) from the cut end using the point of the needle.

② Holding the tail with your free hand, push the needle through to form a neat knot at the eye.

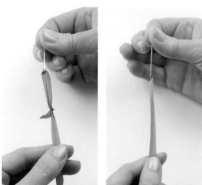

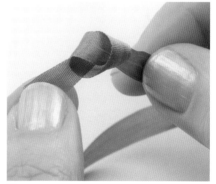

③ Pull the needle with one hand and hold the ribbon taut with the other. The knot will slide up to the eye of the needle.

④ Make a small knot at the other end of the ribbon. Attach wider ribbons to fabric with needle and thread.

Lifting and turning the ribbon

This simple but important technique will guarantee good results.

① Pull the ribbon through the fabric.

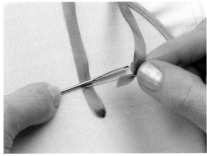

③ To create loops and curls, use a spare needle to control the ribbon while stitching.

② Using a spare needle, gently lift and spread the ribbon open at the entry point. Getting this taut and wrinkle-free may take some practice.

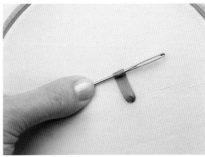

④ Wrap the ribbon evenly around the spare needle, making sure to keep it smooth.

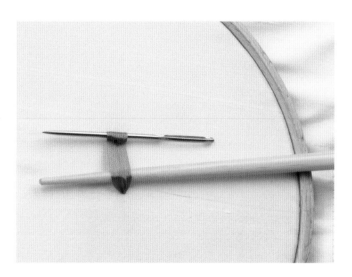

Creating height
Additional height can be created by using a chopstick as a tool to slide beneath the ribbon.

Fastening off
Using a fine needle and a thread that matches your fabric, fasten off your work. The ribbon should be secure and not in danger of unraveling.

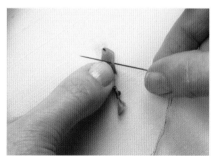

① Whenever possible, after completing a stitch, fasten the ribbon to the back of the fabric using a spare needle and thread.

② Oversew the ribbon neatly in place.

Fabrics

Almost any fabric is suitable for ribbon embroidery, but those most often used include pure linen, silk in a variety of weights and textures, pure cotton, and aida. The fabric should be firm enough to support the stitching, with a weave loose enough for the ribbon to pass through easily. For a good balance of texture and color, the fabric should become an integral part of the design.

Homespun/calico

Homespun/calico
This inexpensive cotton fabric with a smooth finish is often used for soft furnishings. It is available in many different weights, and is ideal if you want to dye or paint the background fabric before embroidering.

Linen

Linen
Pure linen is a plain-weave fabric that is available in a variety of weights. It is used for many types of embroidery, but it creases easily so should be treated with care. Wash the linen to shrink it before you start to embroider.

Canvas

Canvas
Good quality canvas is strong and free of knots, with smooth threads that will not snag the stitches. Fiber canvases are treated with size to stiffen them and should not be dampened until stitching is complete.

Cotton

Cotton
Pure cotton fabric is easy to sew and launder, and is ideal for the novice embroiderer. Light- to medium-weight cottons are relatively inexpensive and work well. It is best to pre-shrink cotton fabric.

Striped canvas

Dyed silks

Hardanger
24-count

Silk

Interface fine silk
fabrics like China silk
or crêpe de Chine
before embroidering.
Silk dupioni is often
used for ribbon
embroidery.
It is woven using silk
from double cocoons
and has a thick,
uneven texture.

Aida
14-count

Hardanger
22-count

Pure silk

Aida with gold
metallic thread

Aida and
hardanger fabric

Available in many
colors, these fabrics are
popular with cross-stitch
embroiderers. The open weave
of the intersecting threads makes
them ideal for ribbon embroidery.
They are available in "counts" of
8 to 18 squares (pairs of threads).
Hardanger fabric comes in 22- or
24-count.

Preparing the Fabric

Before you work ribbon embroidery for a garment, make sure that both fabric and ribbon are colorfast. Pre-wash linen or cotton fabrics to shrink the fibers before you use them for garments or soft furnishings.

Washing silk fabrics
Always use the gentlest detergent when washing silk.

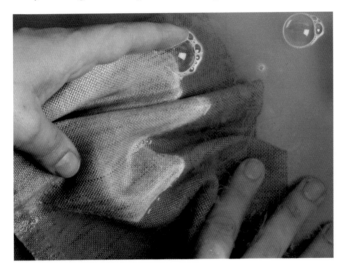

① Immerse the fabric (suiting silk is shown here) in a solution of warm water and mild, pure detergent. Rinse in clean water and allow to air dry.

② Press using a warm iron to straighten the grain of the fabric. Do this before attempting any stitching.

Strengthening fabrics

It is best to strengthen and stabilize lightweight fabrics before use by tacking or fusing lightweight interfacing to the wrong side. Muslin or fine woven interfacing is ideal as it adds body to the fabric; nonwoven dressmakers' interfacing can make it too stiff and difficult to manage. If you use "iron-on" interfacing, follow the manufacturer's instructions.

Cut the interfacing to the same size as the fabric and bond it to the wrong side, following the manufacturer's instructions. If this involves steaming through a damp cloth, leave the fabric flat to dry completely.

Cutting fabric and canvas

Use dressmakers' shears, or large, sharp scissors.

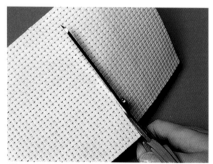

① Any fabric or canvas is normally cut "straight with the grain," that is, along the straight lines of the woven threads (unless, of course, you are cutting a curved shape).

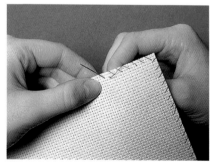

② To avoid frayed edges, overcast around the edge with ordinary sewing thread, or machine stitch with a wide zigzag.

Frames

Many different types of embroidery hoops and frames are used for ribbon embroidery, including wooden, plastic, stretcher, and free-standing slate frames. Better quality frames tend to hold the fabric taut more effectively, but if cost is an issue, wooden hoops are inexpensive and perfectly satisfactory.

Types of embroidery hoops

Embroidery hoops come in a variety of shapes and sizes. If possible, choose a size that will hold the complete design, so the hoop will not need repositioning as work progresses.

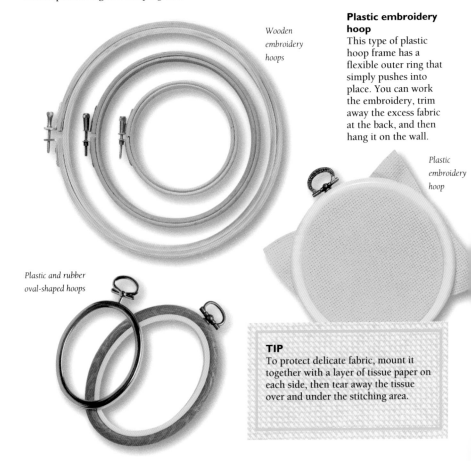

Wooden embroidery hoops

Plastic embroidery hoop

This type of plastic hoop frame has a flexible outer ring that simply pushes into place. You can work the embroidery, trim away the excess fabric at the back, and then hang it on the wall.

Plastic embroidery hoop

Plastic and rubber oval-shaped hoops

TIP
To protect delicate fabric, mount it together with a layer of tissue paper on each side, then tear away the tissue over and under the stitching area.

Stretching over an embroidery hoop

To protect the fabric and stop it slipping, bind the inner ring with cotton bias tape. Place the inner ring flat and lay the fabric over it, right side up, smoothing out the grain. Release the screw on the outer ring gradually, until it fits snugly over the fabric and inner ring. Make sure the fabric is evenly taut.

① Consisting of two wooden rings, simple embroidery hoops have an outer adjustable ring to allow for different weights of fabric.

③ Push the outer ring gently into place. It should fit firmly, holding the fabric flat and taut. If it won't fit, loosen the screw slightly.

② Adjust the size of the hoop's outer ring by means of the screw, so that it fits quite snugly over the inner ring. Lay the inner ring on a flat surface with the fabric centered on top.

④ The finished product. Never, however, leave your work mounted in the hoop when you are not working on it, because the hoop may leave permanent marks on the fabric.

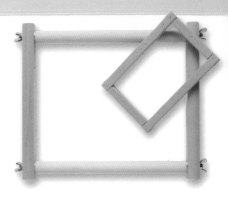

Slate frames

These are available as simple lap frames, or as freestanding frames that leave both hands free to work. Stretch the fabric between the top and bottom rollers by pinning or stitching it to the webbing attached to the rollers. Adjust the rollers to take up the extra fabric. Make sure you stretch enough fabric to accommodate the design, plus a border to mount the completed work.

① Mark the center of the webbing on each roller and match this to the fabric's center. Pin the edge of the fabric to the webbing. Use sewing needle and thread to overcast the fabric edge to webbing on both rollers.

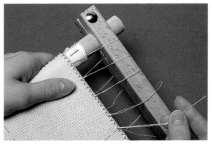

③ With large embroideries, it is a good idea to lace the side edges to the side bars with strong thread—the fabric edges may be temporarily reinforced by sewing on lengths of cotton tape if necessary.

② Wind and stretch the fabric to be embroidered between the rollers. Tighten roller wing nuts.

Stretcher frame

For larger designs, or pieces worked in stages, artists' stretcher frames are useful. Stretch the fabric evenly over the frame, and hold it in place along each side using thumbtacks or staples.

Needles

Needles are graded using a numbering system: The higher the number, the smaller the needle. For ribbon embroidery, make sure the eye is large enough to take the ribbon when it is spread flat. If it is folded or crushed, the edges of the ribbon may be damaged and the quality of work will suffer. The eyes of crewel, chenille, and tapestry needles are large enough to accommodate various widths of ribbon and decorative threads.

1 Stiletto or awl needles

A stiletto is a sharp, pointed tool used to pierce holes in fabric. In ribbon embroidery, a stiletto is often used to make an entry or exit hole for the needle. Silk and organza ribbons are quite fragile, and the less stress placed on them, the better the quality of stitching. A large chenille needle may be used instead of a stiletto.

2 Chenille needles

Chenille needles have a large eye, a thick shaft, and a sharp point. They are usually supplied in packs of mixed sizes 13 to 26. It is important to use the correct size for the width of ribbon.

3 Tapestry needles

Tapestry needles have blunt tips and are available in sizes 13 to 26. In ribbon embroidery, they are used to work stitches that pass between a ribbon stitch and the base fabric. The blunt tip stops the ribbon splitting or catching the fibers.

4 Crewel needles

Crewel needles have a long, slender eye and a fine point. They are generally used to work stranded thread or embroidery thread, but sizes 1 to 3 may be used for very narrow ribbon.

5 Embroidery needles

Embroidery needles come in a wide assortment of sharps, and have long eyes that are particularly well suited to adding embroidered embellishments.

6 Beading needle

Beading needles are used to attach beads to fabric and are very fine and flexible. The eye of the needle is the same width as the shaft.

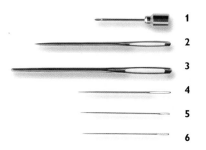

Additional Equipment

Many simple household items make useful tools for ribbon embroidery. Use a toothpick or a chopstick to help to control formation of a stitch (*see page 59, Looped Straight Stitch*). A square of latex cut from a balloon will help to grip the needle when you are using thick or closely woven fabric, such as velvet. Make a simple light box from a cardboard box placed over a lamp with a piece of glass over the opening (*see page 30, Transferring Images*).

TIPS
•To prevent ribbon creasing, wrap it around empty cardboard tubes or containers, or empty sewing spools.
•A good quality steam iron is invaluable for ironing ribbons and fabric, and for reviving tired-looking ribbon embroidery (*see page 44*).

1 Stiff card for stretching finished work
2 Pincushion for pins and needles
3 Thimble to protect fingers
4 Transfer pencils and eraser
5 Sketch pad, ruler, and colored pens
or pencils (for designing)
6 Good quality embroidery scissors
7 Beads for extra decoration
8 Paintbrushes
9 Fabric paints

10 Clear, or masking, tape for tacking fabric
11 Chopstick for use as a ribbon wrapping aid
12 Toothpick
13 Novelty threads for embellishment
14 Light box for transferring designs
15 Cardboard tube (*see Tip, opposite*)
16 A pair of scissors
17 Fabric pens to mark fabric or add detail
18 Fabric paint liners to outline or decorate

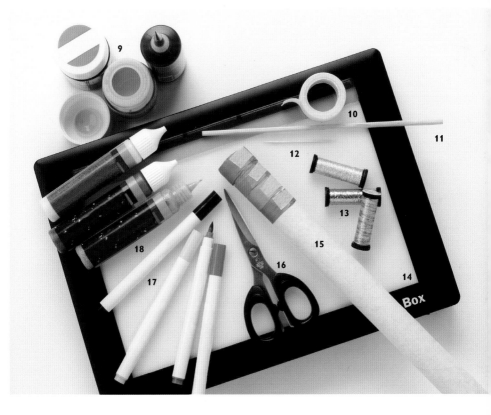

Transferring Images

There are many useful products for transferring designs to fabric, including iron-on transfers, water-soluble markers, transfer markers that fade, dressmakers' chalk or carbon, light boxes, and water-soluble fabric. Whichever you choose, make sure the outline can be erased easily, or that it will be completely covered with stitching.

Equipment needed

1 Light box
2 Water-soluble transfer fabric
3 Carbon paper
4 Tracing grid
5 Transfer pen
6 Transfer pencils
7 Tracing wheel

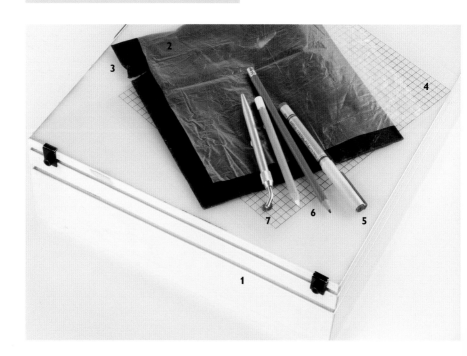

Using dressmakers' carbon

Dressmakers' carbon works in the same way as ordinary carbon paper. It comes in a variety of colors.

① Place the fabric on a flat surface, right side up, and place a sheet of dressmakers' carbon over it, carbon side down. Center the design on the carbon.

② Trace carefully over the image using a fine-tipped pencil or thick needle.

Using a light box

Direct tracing of the design onto the fabric with the use of a light box is probably the simplest method of transfer for transparent materials. Electric or battery-operated light boxes are available in various sizes.

Place the design on the box, right side up. Place the fabric over the box so the design is lit from beneath and shows through the fabric. Trace the design using a transfer marker or, for dark fabric, white chalk. Some embroiderers use a tracing wheel that runs a line of fine-pierced holes through the fabric.

Iron-on ribbon embroidery transfers

In this technique, the pattern is transferred permanently onto the fabric with the use of a heated iron, and therefore must be completely covered by stitching. Always be careful to ensure that your ribbon is wide enough to cover all transfer marks.

① Cut around the transfer leaving plenty of spare paper at the edges. Pin the transfer by the corners, ink side down, where required on the fabric. Place the iron over the transfer area and leave on for about 10 seconds. Do not move the iron around as this may blur the transferred lines. Avoid ironing over the pins.

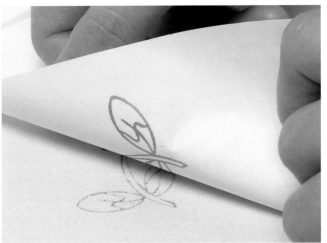

② Carefully lift one corner of the transfer to see if the design has transferred. If not, press again for a longer time, and/or increase the heat setting of the iron. When the design has transferred successfully, remove the transfer paper and work your embroidery.

Using soluble fabric and markers

Another option is to trace your design directly onto water-soluble fabric with markers. After the completion of your piece, immerse your fabric in cold water to remove any trace of the inked pattern from your material.

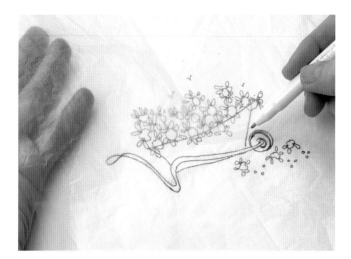

① Place the design under the soluble fabric and trace over it using a water-soluble marker.

② Center the fabric with the traced design over the embroidery fabric and stretch them evenly in a hoop. Stitch through both layers of fabric. Immerse the completed embroidery in water to dissolve the soluble fabric.

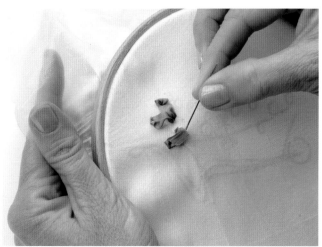

Creating Backgrounds

It is fun to create textures or backgrounds using printing, stamping, appliqué, painting, padding, and freestyle embroidery techniques. Sprinkle rock salt on painted backgrounds while they are wet for interesting effects. Work a cottage or garden scene on the background fabric using stranded thread as a setting for flower embroidery.

Stenciling

Virtually anything that masks off an area of background can be described as a stencil. Buy ready-made stencils or cut your own using heavy paper and a craft knife. Use masking tape to secure the stencil to the fabric.

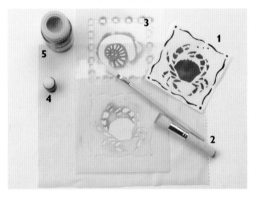

Equipment needed

1 Stenciled sample shows you the finished product

2 Stencil brush and ordinary paintbrush

3 Plastic stencil for outlines that will stay crisp and sharp

4 Stenciling dauber for subtle color transfer

5 Fabric paint transfers a more opaque color onto the fabric

① Lay your stencil in the desired position and secure with masking tape. Gently tap the dauber tip over the area to be colored. Repeat until you have achieved the desired intensity.

② Carefully peel up the masking tape and clear plastic template to check your design for color and coverage. Make sure that the dauber has successfully transferred the entire design.

Printed fabric

Printing on fabric is simple, and craft shops sell a wide range of rubber, polymer, and sponge stamps. To use, apply ink to the stamp, then press it onto the fabric. For the best results, choose fabric with a smooth texture.

Painting fabric

Natural fibers give the best result, but any fabric can be painted. Some fabric paints are translucent, some opaque; all can be diluted with water. Test a small amount on a hidden area before painting the whole fabric.

① A clean, clear canvas is essential for successful fabric painting, so always wash and iron your fabric before you stretch it over your embroidery hoop.

③ For a watercolor effect, add a second, complementary color to the first. If you desire a multihued backdrop, add more colors while the fabric is still wet.

② Use a diluted paint to get a good wash for a background. Wetting the fabric before applying any paint will help avoid unsightly tidemarks in your background wash.

④ The finished backdrop adds to the beauty of the overall ribbon embroidery design. With a little experimenting, you can produce pieces of stunning quality every time.

Appliqué

To add dimension or texture, glue or sew lace, motifs, and contrasting fabrics to the background fabric before embroidering (*see Seashell, page 168, or Climbing Flowers, page 162*). Bonding web, attached to tracing paper, is often use for appliqué.

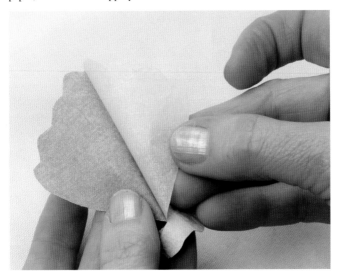

①️ Place the bonding web adhesive-side up over the design and trace with a pencil or fabric marker. Cut out the shape carefully and place it adhesive-side down on the right side of the fabric.

②️ Press evenly with a steam iron set to the correct heat setting for the fabric. Be sure to pass the iron over the entire shape.

③️ Embellish your appliqué design with outlining in decorative dimensional paint to delineate the three-dimensional textures within your simplified, cut-out shape.

Padding

For a three-dimensional effect, stitch felt shapes to the background, and then embroider over the top (*see Lilac in Springtime, page 240*).

Cut a piece of felt the same size and shape as the appliqué motif, then several more, each slightly smaller than the previous. Stitch the smallest to the fabric, then each of the larger ones on top. Finish by stitching wadding to this background shape and then stitch the largest shape on top of that.

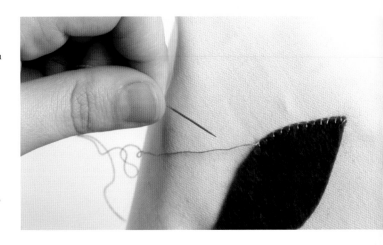

Spraying with fabric paints

A gentle, diffused effect that makes a lovely background can be achieved using a plant spray and fabric paint diluted with water.

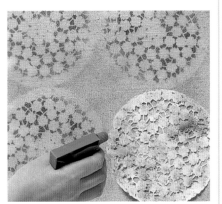

Freestyle embroidery

Indicate space and dimension by stitching an image to the background before adding embroidered embellishments (*see Country Garden, page 244*).

Dyeing Silk Ribbon

Unbleached silk ribbon is available in a variety of widths. Those most readily available are 2mm, 4mm, 7mm, and 13mm, but you can also obtain 32mm. It can be colored using silk or fabric dye, but remember to check the manufacturers' instructions. Use a hair dryer if you wish to speed up the drying process. Press with a warm iron to set the dye and make it colorfast. Follow one of the two methods below to dye the ribbon. The examples were colored using silk dye.

Dyeing in a bowl

① Press the creases out of the ribbon using a warm iron.

③ Immerse the ribbon in the dye and swirl it around using a chopstick.

② Mix the dye in a glass bowl. Add more water to produce pastel colors. Test on a scrap of ribbon and let dry. Colors appear darker when wet.

④ Remove from the dye and hang the ribbon to dry by its end from a drying rack, or tack lengths to a picture frame.

Paint-dyeing ribbons

① Stretch the ribbons over a frame. Make sure they are taut, yet not so tight that the tension causes the thumbtacks to rip holes in the ribbon ends.

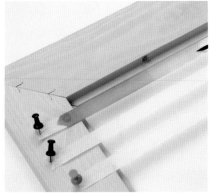

③ To lighten the tint, dilute color with clean water. This can create a wonderful, gradated color across the entire ribbon.

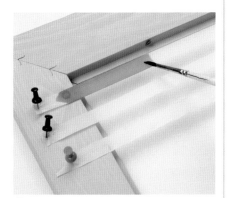

② Paint the lengths of ribbon using a brush. Be careful not to load too much paint on your brush. Consider this a thin wash only.

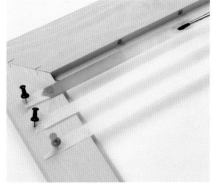

④ For variegated effects, paint on different colors or strengths of color and let them blend while still wet. Let dry, then press with a warm iron to set the dye.

Mounting

Mounting means stretching the finished embroidery before framing. Make sure that the warp and the weft of the fabric are stretched evenly. The work may be stretched over acid-free board. This is the type of board that is used when framing watercolors or photographs, and it is an inexpensive and simple way to mount fabric. The fabric may be laced across the back of the board using a needle and thread, or stuck to the back of the board using mounting tape. As an alternative, pin or staple the work to the back of a wooden stretcher.

Mounting on a board

① Work a neat hem around the edges of the embroidered fabric, either by hand or using a sewing machine. Cut a piece of acid-free board to fit the back of the frame. Place the embroidered fabric on a flat surface, right side down, and center the board over it. Tape or pin the fabric to the edges of the board to hold it in place.

TIP
Keep thread on the spool to ensure you have enough for the entire board.

② Working from the middle out to each end, lace two sides together using a needle and strong thread. Fasten off using Back Stitch (*see page 126*).

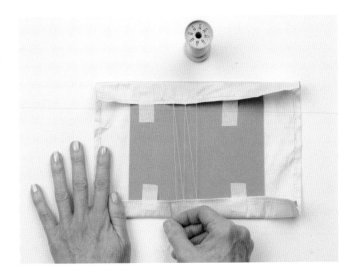

③ Fold the corners into neat squares. Repeat the process for the remaining two sides.

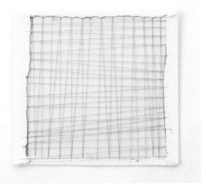

④ Turn the work over and check that the fabric is stretched evenly. Adjust the lacing, then fasten off.

Framing

When framing ribbon embroidery, choose a box or stepped frame to protect the ribbon folds and loops from crushing. This type of frame is often used for different forms of multidimensional craft. It has a wooden or plastic insert that creates space between the mount and the front of the frame. If you use glass, choose the nonreflective type so the effect of your finished work is not spoiled.

Using ready-made mounts

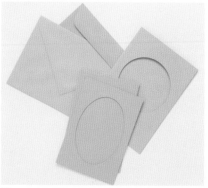

① Consider framing your embroidery as a greeting card. Craft stores have an array of greeting card-style frames including aperture ovals, circles, squares, and rectangles.

② The finished product is a unique, professional-quality card that can be sent to friends and family.

Preparing your work to put into a box frame

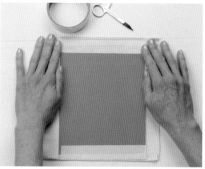

① Work a neat hem around the edge of the embroidered fabric and cut a piece of acid-free board to fit inside the frame. Place the embroidered fabric right side down on a flat surface. Center the board over the back of the fabric. Use double-sided tape to stretch the fabric evenly, attaching it to the back of the board.

② Fold the corners into neat squares.

Using a box frame

① Follow the instructions opposite, then cut a piece of acid-free board to fit the back of the frame. Attach it using double-sided tape.

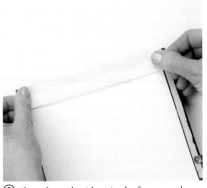

③ Place the embroidery in the frame, and place the thin card behind it. Secure the back of the mount to the frame using acid-free mounting tape.

② Cut a thin piece of card to cover the back of the board.

④ The box-framed card has now become a beautiful piece of art to adorn your wall.

Care of Finished Pieces

Ribbon embroidery can be used for cards, framed pictures, or decorative work on household and personal articles. If it is to be used on a garment, wash both garment and ribbon first to make sure they are colorfast. If you are using knitted fabric, it may be best to apply interfacing to the wrong side before placing it in the hoop, to prevent it from stretching. Linen or pure cotton fabric should always be pre-shrunk before stitching. Ribbon embroidered garments should be dry cleaned, or hand-washed using mild detergent.

Steaming

Repeated handling may flatten ribbon embroidery, but woven ribbon, like woven fabric, has a "memory." To lift and refresh work, hold a steam iron 6–9 in. (15–23cm) above it and steam for a few seconds. Do not allow the iron to touch the ribbon. Lift the flattened loops and stitches gently using a needle. Support the ribbon with a chopstick until it is cool.

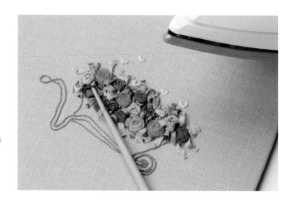

Spritzing

① To clean and revive crushed or soiled stitches simply blow away the dust gently using a hair dryer set to cool.

② Make sure the ribbon is colorfast, then "spritz" it using a hand spray and a very fine mist of water. Do not saturate the work. Lift the loops and stitches using a spare needle, and then place them gently back in the desired shape. Let dry.

Packaging

Always mail ribbon embroidery designs in boxes, and support them using bubblewrap or tissue to prevent them from being crushed in the mail. When transporting them, make a temporary frame using one of the methods right and below.

Styrofoam Cut out the middle of a piece of styrofoam and place the embroidery in the center of the cut out. Several designs may be stacked on top of each other using this technique.

Tissue and bubblewrap
Place a piece of tissue paper over the design. Tear a hole in the center large enough to expose the motif. Roll strips of bubblewrap into tubes, and attach to the edges of the tissue paper with clear tape.

Stitch Collection

This section will enable you to follow patterns produced by designers to create beautiful and individual motifs. More than 60 popular stitches and combinations of stitches are described using simple, easy-to-follow steps and diagrams. To ensure good stitch quality, make sure the stitches are longer than your chosen ribbon is wide, and allow the ribbon to spread.

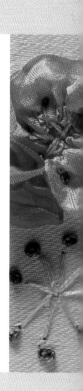

Ribbon Stitch Selector

The Ribbon Stitch Selector provides a quick reference
to the stitches contained in the Stitch Collection. The
stitches are divided into families, and an illustration of
each stitch is included.

Straight Stitches

Straight or line stitches
are often used to
represent linear elements
in a design, such as a
flower stalk. They are
also used to add detail,
or to create borders and
patterns. Combine them
with different stitches to
create specific flowers
and leaves.

page 58   *Straight Stitch*

page 59   *Looped Straight Stitch*

page 60   *Twisted Straight Stitch*

page 61   *Padded Straight Stitch*

Detached Stitches

Detached stitches have many uses. They are often combined with other stitches, particularly for floral work. Work them in a regular pattern, or scatter them informally. A single stitch, such as a Detached Chain Stitch, is ideal for a feature such as a flower petal.

page 62   *Fly Stitch*

page 63   *Ribbon Stitch*

page 64   *Grab Stitch*

page 65   *Detached Chain Stitch*

page 66   *Twisted Detached Chain Stitch*

page 67   *Loop Stitch Bow*

page 68   *Ribbon Filler Stitch*

Knots

Colonial and French Knots are used to represent an element of a design, such as an eye or as the center of a flower. The size of the knot depends upon the width of the ribbon used. Work knots singly, in a regular pattern to create texture, or scatter them to fill spaces.

page 69 *Colonial Knot*

page 70 *French Knot*

Combined Stitches

Ribbon embroidery is very different from other forms of embroidery. With imagination, plus experimentation and practice, it is possible to represent almost anything. Most images are worked using different combinations of stitches, and varying the type and width of ribbon used expands the possibilities still further.

page 71 *Bullion Knot & Detached Chain Stitch*

page 72 *Detached Chain & Straight Stitch*

page 73 *Running Stitch & Colonial Knot*

Linked and Woven Stitches

Linked stitches may be worked open or closed to create texture or natural forms. Leaves, stems, and seaweed are often worked using Cretan or Chained Feather Stitch. Woven stitches are worked in layers. The first layer is sometimes worked in thread, then the ribbon is woven between the strands. They are ideal for baskets or for a solid area such as a garden wall in a floral design.

page 74   *Wheatear Stitch*

page 75   *Fern Stitch*

page 76   *Chained Feather Stitch*

page 77   *Ribbon Weaving*

page 78   *Cretan Stitch*

page 79   *Open Cretan Stitch*

page 80   *Chevron Stitch*

page 81   *Fishbone Stitch*

page 82   *Herringbone Stitch*

page 83   *Open Chain Stitch*

Decorative Stitches

The freestyle stitches in this collection will add texture and interest to ribbon embroidery designs. They may be worked using embroidery thread or narrow ribbon. Some, such as Star Stitch, can be worked alone; others, such as Satin Stitch, can be used to fill in a space. Use Couching techniques for stems or bows, or to outline objects. Other decorative stitches, such as Rosette Chain Stitch, are ideal for motifs or fancy borders.

page 84 — *Satin Stitch*

page 85 — *Couching*

page 86 — *Star Stitch*

page 87 — *Upright Cross Stitch*

page 88 — *Rosette Chain Stitch*

Flowers and Leaves

Almost any kind of flower—real or imaginary—may be worked in ribbon embroidery. Flowers may be created using a single stitch, a combination of stitches, or by weaving, folding, twirling, gathering, and layering. Padding adds an extra dimension. For stamens and calyxes, use Colonial or French Knots, Bullion Stitch, Twisted Straight Stitch, and Grab Stitch. Leaves and foliage can be worked using either thread or ribbon and linked, straight, chain, twisted, or gathered stitches. Ribbon Stitch (*see page 63*) is also a common leaf stitch—the width of the ribbon used determines the size of the leaf.

page 89   *Ribbon Leaf*

page 90   *Gathered Leaf*

page 91   *Flower Buds*

page 92   *Gathered Ribbon Flower*

page 93   *Scrunched Gathered Flower*

page 94   *Stem Stitch*

page 95   *Stamens*

page 96   *Pansy*

Flowers and Leaves continued

page 97   *Snowdrop*

page 98   *Primrose*

page 99   *Closed Iris*

page 100   *Lily*

page 101   *Daisy*

page 102   *Ivy*

page 103   *Holly*

page 104   *Pine Cone*

page 105 Basic Fuchsia

page 106 Chinese Lantern

page 107 Bleeding Heart

page 108 Cattail

Roses

Make ribbon roses using folding, gathering, weaving, and twisting techniques. Work them straight onto the fabric, or make them separately and attach them using a needle and thread (*see page 111, Concertina Rose*). The wider the ribbon, the bigger the rose. French Knots and beads may be used to enhance the center.

page 109   *Rosebud*

page 110   *Padded Rosebud*

page 111   *Concertina Rose*

page 112   *Spider Web Rose*

page 113   *Folded Ribbon Rose*

page 114   *Twirled Ribbon Rose*

Insects, Birds, and Animals

Animals and insects may be worked in a combination of stitches, or using a single detached stitch such as Fly Stitch (*see page 62*). Ribbon width is important; if it is too wide, the design may look bulky and unattractive. Details including eyes, mouths, wings, and gills may be added using embroidery thread.

page 115   *Parrot*

page 116   *Dragonfly*

page 117   *Sheep*

page 118   *Fish*

page 119   *Butterfly*

Straight Stitch

One of the simplest stitches used in silk
ribbon embroidery, Straight Stitch has a
variety of applications and uses. It may
be used to create petals, leaves, and
flowers, and is also used for monograms,
insects, and other images. It may be
worked in any direction.

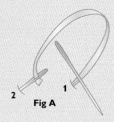

| 13mm | 7mm | 4mm | 2mm |

Method

Fig A Bring the needle up at **1**, keeping the
ribbon flat. Take the needle through to the
back of the fabric at **2**, controlling the entry
and exit points of the stitch with a spare
needle. Fasten the ribbon at the back using
needle and thread.

2   1

Fig A

Note Illustrated as ◀▬▶ in Motif Library.
Uses Flowers, petals, and detailing. Also used
to give volume to Padded Straight Stitch (*see
page 61*).

Looped Straight Stitch

Straight stitches may be flat, twisted, or
looped. It is important to control the entry
and exit points of the stitch, as the ribbon
behaves differently at each point. Petals may
be stitched from the center out to the tip, or
from the tip in to the center. Looped Straight
Stitch is usually worked with other stitches, to
create a variety of different petals and leaves.
In the example, right, a French Knot (*see page
70*) is worked through its center.

13mm   **7mm**   **4mm**   **2mm**

Method

Fig A Fasten the ribbon at the back. Bring
the needle up at **1**. Take the needle through
to the back of the fabric at **2**, controlling the
entry and exit points of the stitch with a
spare needle.

Fig B Place a toothpick or chopstick under
the ribbon loop and pull the loop against it.

Fig C Fasten the loop at the back of the fabric.

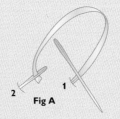

2   **1**
Fig A

Fig B

Fig C

Notes Stitching through ribbons on the underside
of the fabric will distort the petals. Work the petals
around the center of the flower at the back of the
fabric. To create this petal, use French Knots (*see*
page 70) in the middle of each loop. Illustrated as
🌑 in Motif Library.

Uses For flowers such as daisy, aster, buttercup,
and jonquil.

Twisted Straight Stitch

Twisted Straight Stitch is used to create stems, leaves, and petals, and to add decorative ribbon twirls to many silk ribbon motifs. It can be very useful for indicating movement, such as the stems of cattails blown in the wind. It may be worked in many different widths of ribbon to various lengths, and in any direction.

13mm   7mm   4mm   2mm

Method

Fig A Fasten the ribbon at the back of the fabric. Bring it up at **1**, holding it above the fabric with finger and thumb.

Fig B Twist the ribbon once, twice, or several times, depending on the effect required, and hold the twists with finger and thumb. Take the point of the needle down at **2**, and fasten the stitch at the back.

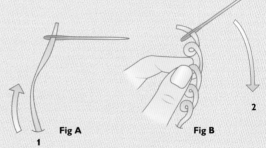

Fig A   1   Fig B   2

Notes Interesting effects may be created by using transparent organza or variegated ribbons. Illustrated as ●━● in Motif Library.
Uses This stitch is combined with other stitches.

For example, it may be worked several times to create a flower head before stems and leaves are added using embroidery thread and Straight Stitch (*see page 58*).

Padded Straight Stitch

As its name implies, Padded Straight Stitch is a double-layered stitch that is used to add volume and depth to a design. It is easy to vary the colors and shades of petals and leaves; try working Padded Straight Stitch using silk ribbon in a solid color, then use organza ribbon in a different color for the overlay. The effect of the finished stitch will be completely different. The stitch may be lifted with a toothpick or chopstick to add height (*see Looped Straight Stitch, page 59*), or worked as shown.

| 13mm | 7mm | 4mm | 2mm |

Method

Fig A Fasten the ribbon at the back of the fabric. Bring the needle up at **1**, form a loop, then take it back down through the fabric at **2**.

Fig B Bring the needle back up at **3**, just above **1**.

Fig C Keeping the ribbon flat, take it down at **4**.

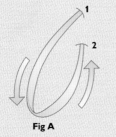

Fig A

Fig B

Fig C

Notes Complete each padded stitch before adding extra stitches, as the ribbon can become quite bulky and spoil the top finish of the fabric. Illustrated as ⬤ in Motif Library.

Uses This stitch is often used in large floral designs, or to decorate cushion covers and other soft furnishings.

Fly Stitch

Fly Stitch belongs to the detached stitch family, and is one of the easiest to master. It is also used in freestyle embroidery, and can be used to create flies, birds, and flowers, or as a base stitch for woven roses. In the example shown here, it was used for the flower heads. It can be worked as single stitches scattered on a design, or in rows for a border or filling. Ribbons in a variety of widths may be used and the stitch can be worked in any direction.

| 13mm | 7mm | 4mm | 2mm |

Method
Fig A Bring the needle up at **1** and form a loop. Keeping the ribbon flat, take the needle down at **2**. Bring it back up at **3**. The point of the needle lies over the loop of the ribbon.

Fig B Take the needle back down at **4**. Fasten the ribbon off at the back of the fabric.

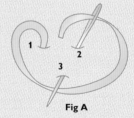

Fig A   **Fig B**

Note Illustrated as 🙵 in Motif Library.
Uses Fly Stitch can be used to make leaves and palm fronds in a row or border. It may also be combined with other stitches: Ribbon Stitch (*see page 63*) and Straight Stitch (*see page 58*) were used for the stem and leaves of the design above.

Ribbon Stitch

Perhaps the most frequently used of ribbon embroidery stitches, Ribbon Stitch can be made using many different widths of ribbon. Its shape can be varied by lifting it with a chopstick, placing a bead beneath it for a padded effect, or by changing the point of entry when creating the curl. It is used in many different images, including flowers, leaves, insects, and birds. It may be worked in any direction.

13mm

7mm

4mm

2mm

Method

Fig A Fasten the ribbon at the back. Bring it up at **1** and hold it down flat against the fabric with your thumb. With a spare needle, carefully lift the point of entry.

Fig B Now place the spare needle, horizontally to the ribbon, where the curl is desired.

Fig C Take the needle down at **2**, through the ribbon, over the horizontal needle, and through to the back of the fabric. Carefully pull the ribbon through the fabric, making sure you do not pull the curl right through. Fasten the stitch off at the back.

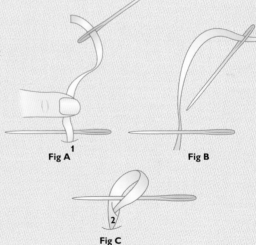

1
Fig A

Fig B

2
Fig C

Note Illustrated as ● in Motif Library.
Uses This stitch is extremely versatile. Use it to create flowers, leaves, animals, and insects. As it can be worked using ribbons of any width, it lends itself to three-dimensional embroidery.

Grab Stitch

Grab Stitch is usually used to make the calyx at the base of a flower or flower bud. Though it is a detached stitch, it is only used with other stitches. It may be worked using various widths of ribbon or in stranded embroidery thread.

13mm   **7mm**   **4mm**   **2mm**

Method

Fig A Create a petal, or bud, for which you wish to make a calyx. Fasten the ribbon off at the back of the fabric and bring the needle up at **1**.

Fig B Make a loop, then take the needle back down at **2**, just to the left of **1**.

Fig C Bring the needle out at **3**, close to the base of the petal, taking care not to pull the loop right through to the back of the fabric.

Fig D Take the needle back through the loop. Pull the loop gently to close.

Fig E Take the needle down at **4** to create a stem.

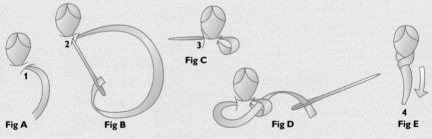

Fig A   Fig B   Fig C   Fig D   Fig E

Note Ribbon Stitch (*see page 63*) was used for the leaves in this design.

Detached Chain Stitch

A traditional stitch that is more usually known as lazy daisy stitch, Detached Chain Stitch may be worked randomly in a motif, or grouped to create flowers or leaves. It is often used to create daisies, irises, and bleeding heart flowers. It may be made in any direction, and the tail or anchoring stitch may be lengthened as desired.

| 13mm | 7mm | 4mm | 2mm |

Method

Fig A Bring the needle up at **1** and form a soft loop. Take the needle down close to **1** and bring it back up at **2**, over the loop of ribbon.

Fig B Take the needle down at **3** to anchor the loop. Fasten the ribbon off at the back of your work. Repeat as required.

Fig C The completed stitch. For an extended Detached Chain Stitch, create a longer tail by taking the entry point **3** further away from the stitch.

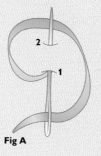
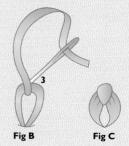

Fig A   Fig B   Fig C

Notes The effect of the stitch will change depending on how tightly or loosely it is worked. Illustrated as **◑** in Motif Library.

Uses A decorative stitch for small, medium, and large flowers and leaves.

Twisted Detached Chain Stitch

A twisted variation of Detached Chain Stitch (*see page 65*) is worked in a similar way, but with the entry and exit points reversed. It can be used to add details to a design, or with other stitches to create effects such as the delicate center of a rosebud or an iris.

13mm

Method

Fig A Fasten the ribbon off at the back of the fabric. Bring the needle up at **1** and hold the ribbon down against the fabric as shown. Take the needle back down at **2**.

Fig B Bring the needle up at **3**, with the point over the top of the ribbon loop. Take the needle down at **4**.

Fig C Fasten the ribbon off at the back of the fabric.

7mm

4mm

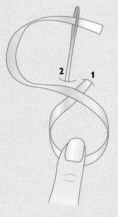

2mm

Fig A   **Fig B**   **Fig C**

Note Different effects may be achieved by changing the length or width, and how tightly or loosely the stitch is worked.

Loop Stitch Bow

This pretty Loop Stitch Bow is worked using an extremely simple stitch. It is useful both in ribbon embroidery, and to embellish freestyle embroidery. It may be used to "tie" a flower bouquet, for ribbon bows in a young girl's hair, or for a bow on a teddy bear's neck. It may be made using ribbons in a variety of widths, and in any direction.

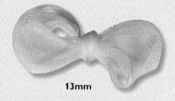

13mm

7mm

4mm

2mm

Method

Fig A Fasten the ribbon at the back of the fabric and bring it up at **1** to form a loop. Take the needle to the back of the fabric at **2**. Keep the ribbon smooth, without any twists.

Fig B Place a finger in the middle of the loop, and press it flat.

Fig C Bring the needle up at **3**, toward the middle and at the back of the loop. Wrap it over the front, and then take it down and through to the back of the fabric at **4**.

Fig D Pull the wrap gently, keeping the ribbon flat until it forms the loop into a bow. Fasten the ribbon at the back of the fabric.

1   2

Fig A

Fig B

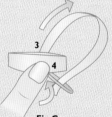

3

4

Fig C

Fig D

Note Illustrated as in Motif Library.

Ribbon Filler Stitch

A purely decorative stitch that is always used with other stitches, Ribbon Filler Stitch is formed by folding and looping lengths of ribbon, then fastening them together at the base of the folds using sewing thread. In the example, right, it forms the inner petals of the flowers. It may be worked using ribbons in a variety of widths. Loops of different lengths can be made, and extra loops may be worked if desired. The completed Ribbon Filler Stitch is attached to the fabric with sewing thread, and its base is covered with stitches.

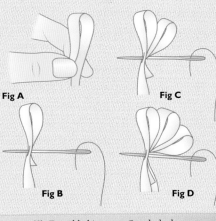

13mm   7mm   4mm   2mm

Method

Fig A Make a loop in a length of ribbon and pinch the ends together at the base.

Fig B Using a needle and thread, stitch through the pinched ends and gather them together.

Fig C Create a second fold. Stitch the second fold to the first at its base.

Fig D Create another fold and then stitch the three folds firmly together at the base. Trim off the ends of the ribbon. Attach the Ribbon Filler to the fabric and work stitches to cover its tail.

Fig A

Fig B

Fig C

Fig D

Uses Ribbon Filler Stitch can be worked as a bow or the center of a flower. It is ideal for three-dimensional work. Loops may be Couched to the fabric with stitches such as Colonial Knots (see page 69). For added interest, Couch the loops to the fabric with small seed or glass beads.

Colonial Knot

The Colonial Knot is used to create detail, or as a decorative stitch. It is worked either scattered over a design or to create a delicate group of flowers. It is similar to a French Knot (*see page 70*) except that the ribbon is wrapped in a figure-eight around the needle before it is stitched to the fabric. Colonial Knots can also be worked with embroidery thread. The width of the ribbon or number of strands of thread used will determine the size of the knot. Wider widths of ribbon are more difficult to manipulate and will create a bulkier shape.

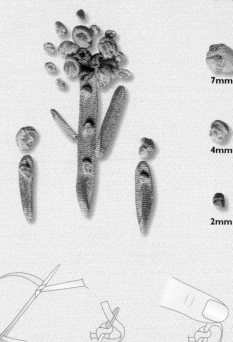

7mm

4mm

2mm

Fig A   **Fig B**   **Fig C**   **Fig D**   **Fig E**

Method

Fig A Fasten the ribbon at the back of the fabric. Bring it up to the surface of the fabric at **1**. Keeping the ribbon flat, place the needle over it at an angle.

Fig B Wrap the point of the needle under the ribbon, where it emerges from the fabric.

Fig C Wrap the ribbon over and under the tip of the needle. Tighten the loop around the needle by pulling the ribbon gently.

Fig D Take the needle point through to the back of the fabric, as close as possible to **1**. Pull

the wraps of ribbon firmly against the needle. Push the needle into the fabric.

Fig E Pull through to the back of the fabric so that a loop forms. Hold the knot and loop on the fabric with your thumb as you continue to pull the ribbon through. Fasten the ribbon off at the back of the fabric.

Note Illustrated as ▦ in Motif Library.

French Knot

For a traditional French Knot, the ribbon is twisted only once around the needle, as this makes a neat knot. In ribbon embroidery, the ribbon may be wound two or more times around the needle to create a variety of different knots. The width of the ribbon and the size of the needle determine the size of the knot. The samples here show extended French Knots.

13mm   **7mm**   **4mm**   **2mm**

Method

Fig A Bring the needle up at **1** and wind the ribbon once or twice around the needle. The ribbon may be twisted or held flat. Hold the ribbon taut with the finger and thumb.

Fig B Place the point of the needle just beside **1**. Pull the needle through to the back of the work at **2** to create a neat knot. Varying the tension will create different knot shapes.

Fig C The finished knot.

Fig D For an extended French Knot, bring the needle up at **1**. Wind the ribbon once or twice around the needle. Take the ribbon down a short distance away at **2**, creating a tail below the knot.

Fig E The finished extended French Knot.

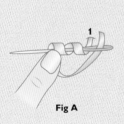  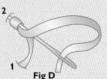

Fig A   **Fig B**   **Fig C**   **Fig D**   **Fig E**

Notes The French Knot is also known as French dot, twisted knot stitch, and knotted stitch. Illustrated as ● in Motif Library.

Uses Suitable for creating texture, French Knots may be used scattered or grouped. Often used for details such as eyes, rosebuds, or the tips of flower stamens.

Bullion Knot & Detached Chain Stitch

A combination of Bullion Knot and Detached Chain Stitch makes an attractive stitch that can be used to create flowers and buds, and may be made in a variety of ribbon widths. It is not too difficult to master, but a beginner may need a little practice. If you are working it for the first time, practice on scrap fabric until you are happy with the result.

13mm

Method

Fig A Fasten the ribbon to the back of the fabric. Bring it up at **1** and lay it flat on the surface. Push the needle through the fabric, just to the right of **1** and bring the point out at **2**. Take the ribbon from left to right and under the point of the needle at **2**.

7mm

Fig B Keeping the ribbon flat, wrap it around the tip of the needle at **3**. Gently pull the ribbon so that it lies snugly against the needle. Wrap the ribbon around the point of the needle at **3** a few more times. The more wraps, the larger the Bullion Knot.

Fig C Holding the wraps in place with your thumb, gently pull the eye of the needle through the wraps at **4**.

4mm

Fig D Pull the ribbon until the wraps form a Bullion Knot at the end of the Detached Chain Stitch. Take the needle to the back of the fabric at **5**, just to the right of the Bullion Knot. Fasten the ribbon at the back of the fabric.

2mm

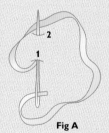

Fig A   **Fig B**   **Fig C**   **Fig D**

Detached Chain & Straight Stitch

Detached Chain Stitch combined with Straight Stitch is an easy and very useful stitch. Its size and width is determined by the width of the ribbons used. This stitch is also suitable for adding details to a design using stranded embroidery threads. It is often used for floral designs, with the center of the chain filled with French Knots (*see page 70*) or other delicate stitches. Stitches may be worked in groups to create an object, or singly to form petals at the end of a row of Stem Stitch (*see page 94*).

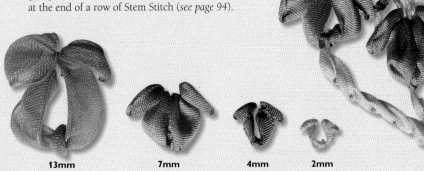

13mm   **7mm**   **4mm**   **2mm**

Method

Fig A Fasten the ribbon at the back of the fabric and bring it to the surface of the fabric at **1**. Take the needle through the fabric, to the right of **1**, to form a loop, and bring the point out at **2**. Keep the ribbon flat and smooth under the point of the needle.

Fig B Take the needle down at **3** to create a chain.

Fig C Bring the ribbon back up at **4** and make a Straight Stitch to the left of the chain, taking the needle down at **5**. Bring it back up at **6**. Make another Straight Stitch and take the needle down at **7**.

Fig D The completed stitch. Fasten the ribbon at the back of the fabric.

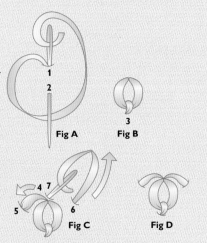

Fig A   **Fig B**

Fig C   **Fig D**

Uses This stitch can be worked using variegated ribbon to make flowers on embroidered stems. Try using it for the head of an Easter bunny with floppy ears, adding French Knot "eyes" and Straight Stitch "whiskers" using stranded thread.

Running Stitch & Colonial Knot

Running Stitch is a basic straight stitch used extensively in both ribbon and freestyle embroidery. In ribbon embroidery, Running Stitch is usually used to outline, or is "whipped" to create a border or trailing stems and vines. Running Stitch is combined here with a Colonial Knot to produce an extremely delicate rose. This combined stitch is slightly difficult and a beginner may need a little practice and patience. Most ribbon widths are suitable, but very narrow 2mm ribbon is more difficult to control.

Running Stitch
Fig A Fasten the ribbon to the back of the fabric. Bring it up at **1** and take it down at **2** to form a Straight Stitch (*see page 58*). Leave a space the width of the ribbon between stitches. Bring the needle up at **3** and take it back down at **4**. Work a line of Running Stitch in this way and fasten the ribbon at the back of the fabric.

Whipped Running Stitch
Fig B Thread a needle with ribbon in the same or a contrasting color. Bring it up just behind the first Running Stitch and pass the needle under the stitch from right to left. Do not stitch through the fabric. Continue to weave through the stitches. Keep the gauge even but fairly loose, and allow the whipped ribbon to twist freely. Fasten the whipped ribbon at the back of the fabric.

Running Stitch & Colonial Knot
Fig C Bring the ribbon up through the fabric at **1**. Work a Colonial Knot (*see page 69*) into the ribbon about 2 in. (5cm) away from **1** at **2**.

Fig D Hold the knot on the needle and turn the needle so the point pierces the 2 in. (5cm) length of ribbon at **3**. Make six or more Running Stitches, each approximately ¼ in. (6mm) long, down the center of the ribbon.

Fig E Insert the needle into the fabric at **4** (close to **1**). Tighten the knot by pulling on the back length of the ribbon. Take the needle through the fabric. Continue to pull the ribbon until it folds up into petals, with a Colonial Knot in the center. Fasten off at the back of the fabric.

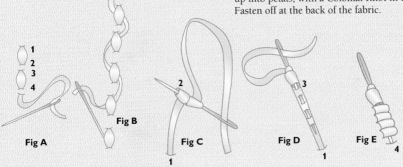

Fig A

Fig B

Fig C

Fig D

Fig E

Note Illustrated as 🌸 in Motif Library.

Wheatear Stitch

When Wheatear Stitch is worked evenly in narrow ribbon it looks like ears of wheat. It is shown here as a linked stitch, but it may also be worked as a detached stitch, or used randomly as a filling or for foliage. To maintain an even gauge, it is best worked in ribbon widths of 2mm, 4mm, or 7mm, or embroidery thread.

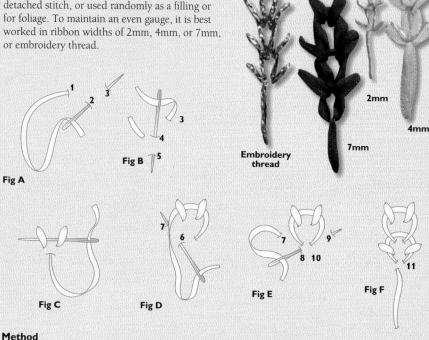

Fig A

Fig B

Fig C

Fig D

Fig E

Fig F

2mm

4mm

7mm

Embroidery thread

Method

Fig A Fasten the ribbon to the back of the fabric. Bring the needle up at **1**. Take it back down through the fabric at **2** and bring it up again at **3**.

Fig B Take the needle down at **4** and back up at **5**, to form two evenly spaced Straight Stitches.

Fig C Pass the needle under the Straight Stitches as shown. Do not pierce the fabric.

Fig D Make a loop by taking the needle back down at **6**. Bring it up again at **7**.

Fig E To link the stitches, make a Straight Stitch (*see page 58*) beginning at **7**, taking the ribbon down at **8**. Bring it back up at **9** and down again at **10**.

Fig F Bring the ribbon up again at **11** and weave the ribbon under the stitches as shown. Continue the sequence until the desired pattern has been worked. Take the ribbon down in a long Straight Stitch to form a stem and fasten at the back.

Note Illustrated as 🐾 in Motif Library.

Fern Stitch

Like Wheatear Stitch, Fern Stitch may be worked as a detached stitch or linked for a fernlike effect. It may be used scattered, or worked in straight and curved lines. Worked detached, it is useful for the stems of small clusters of flowers. It may be made in any direction, and worked in ribbons in a variety of widths. Worked in stranded thread, it makes perfect little claws for birds or chickens.

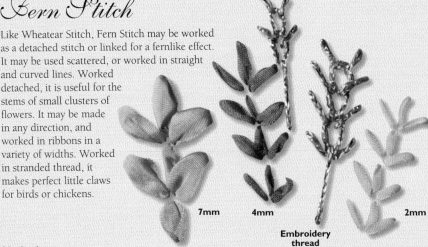

7mm   4mm   2mm

Embroidery thread

Method

Fig A To create a linked row of Fern Stitches, first draw a pattern on the fabric. Fasten the ribbon at the back. Bring it to the surface of the fabric at **1** and make a Straight Stitch (*see page 58*) taking the needle back down at **2**. Keep the ribbon flat and smooth.

Fig B Bring the ribbon up at **3**. Take it back down at **4**, just below **1**.

Fig C Bring the needle back up at **5** and take it down at **6**.

Fig D To form the fern stem, bring the needle up at **7** and take it down at **8**.

Fig E Repeat the pattern as at **9**, **10** and **11** until it is finished. Fasten the ribbon off at the back of the fabric.

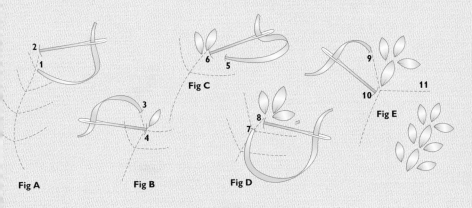

Fig A   Fig B   Fig C   Fig D   Fig E

Uses Work as a linked stitch to indicate a fern. For a shrub, make overlapping stitches using stranded thread. Small ribbon buds and flowers may be stitched at the point of each straight stitch.

To represent seaweed in an underwater design, use ribbon in a variety of widths.

Chained Feather Stitch

Chained Feather Stitch is a linked stitch that is useful for working borders to enclose a motif. The ribbon may be kept flat and smooth, or allowed to twist to add texture and variety to a design. For a border, it is advisable to draw guidelines to maintain the width of chain being made. Use regular, evenly spaced stitches, or vary the size and shape of stitches to create a rambling vine or plant stems.

4mm

2mm

13mm

7mm

7mm

Method

Fig A Fasten the ribbon at the back of the fabric. Bring the needle up at **1** and make a chain. Take the ribbon back down as close as possible to **1**. Bring the needle up again at **2** and lay the ribbon over the center of the chain. Hold it down with your thumb. Take the needle down at **3** to create a chain with a tail. Bring the needle back up at **4** .

Fig B Make another looped chain, taking the needle down as close to **4** as possible. Bring the needle up close to **3** at **5**.

Fig C Take the needle down at **6** and bring it back up at **7**.

Fig D Form another chain by taking the needle down close to **7** and back up close to **6**. Repeat the process, making chains with tails and working from the right to the left of the linked stitches.

Fig E Finish with a tail in Straight Stitch (*see page 58*). Take the needle through to the back of the fabric and fasten off.

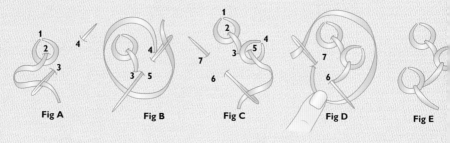

Fig A

Fig B

Fig C

Fig D

Fig E

Notes When using ribbon 13mm wide or more, it is advisable to make a hole in the fabric before stitching through with the threaded ribbon. This prevents pulls in the fabric.

Illustrated as 8 in Motif Library.

Ribbon Weaving

For Ribbon Weaving, the warp thread is made using either a decorative thread or a stranded thread that matches the color of the ribbons. The color of the ribbon used for the weft may be changed to create different effects, and it is particularly effective worked in multicolored ribbon. Ribbon Weaving may be used to produce effects including basketwork, window panes, the roof of a thatched cottage, or a brick wall. It may also be combined with other stitches. It may be stitched in any direction, and the weaving pattern may be varied to suit the chosen design. It is important to keep the gauge even. Control the entry and exit points of the ribbon with a separate needle to prevent twisting.

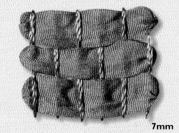

7mm

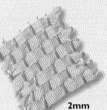

2mm

4mm

Method

Fig A Mark the width and depth of your pattern before you start to stitch. Using either a decorative or matching embroidery thread, sew the warp stitches. Bring the needle and thread up at **1** and back down at **2**. Bring it up at **3**, take it down and back through the fabric at **4**. Repeat the process until the desired depth is achieved.

Fig B Fasten the ribbon to the back of the fabric. Bring the needle and ribbon up at **1**.

Pass the needle under the first warp thread without piercing the fabric, and then take it over the second. Repeat the process to the end.

Fig C Take the needle down at **2** and back up at **3**. Continue to weave in and out of the warp threads, keeping the ribbon flat and even. The sides of the weft ribbons should touch but not overlap. Continue until the weaving is finished. Take the needle to the back of the fabric and fasten.

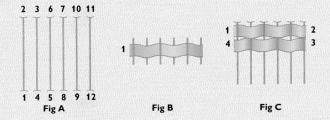

Fig A

Fig B

Fig C

Cretan Stitch

Cretan Stitch is a linked stitch with a braided formation in the center. It is often used to create leaves. It may be worked as an open stitch for a border, or more closely for a textured effect. It is an excellent stitch for suggesting movement, as it may be curved to the right, left, up, or down. With a little imagination, and a variety of colored ribbons and embroidery threads, it could be used to represent waves in the sea, sand dunes, or a stream running through a garden or fields.

4mm   2mm

7mm

Method

Fig A Draw an outline of the shape you wish to embroider. Bring the needle up at **1**. Take it down at **2** and bring the point back up at **3**. Loop the ribbon under the needle. Pull the needle all the way through the fabric.

Fig B Take the needle down at **4** and bring it back up at **5**. Loop the ribbon under the needle. Pull the needle through.

Fig C Take the needle down at **6** and bring it back up at **7**. Loop the ribbon under the needle. Pull the needle through.

Fig D Continue the process until finished. Take the ribbon to the back of the fabric and fasten off.

Fig E The completed leaf.

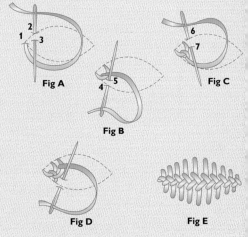

Open Cretan Stitch

Open Cretan Stitch belongs to the decorative feather stitch family, and is often used for ferns in garden designs. It may also be used for a decorative border. The width and distance between stitches may be varied. The examples here show 2mm, 4mm, and 7mm ribbon. The bulk of the stitch means that wider ribbon is unsuitable, unless the design being worked is particularly large and open.

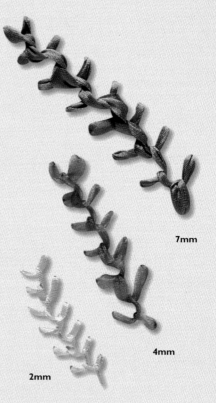

Method

Fig A Draw guidelines for your border. Bring the needle up at **1**. Take it down at **2** and bring it back up at **3**. Make sure the ribbon is lying flat under the point of the needle at **3**. Pull the needle through the fabric to create a flat stitch.

Fig B Take the needle down at **4** and bring it back up at **5**. Make sure the point is lying over the ribbon. Pull the needle through. Continue to the desired length, working stitches alternately up and down.

7mm

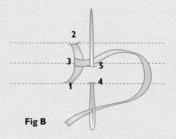

4mm

2mm

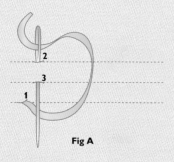

Fig A

Fig B

Note Weave contrasting ribbon through the linked stitches to create a more decorative border.

Chevron Stitch

Chevron Stitch is useful as a border or filling stitch. Because its width and height may be varied, it is often used to decorate garments, such as the cuffs or bodice of a blouse or nightdress. It may be combined with other embroidery stitches to create a variety of interesting patterns. To maintain control of its shape, it is most often worked in 2mm and 4mm ribbon. These examples show 7mm, 4mm, and 2mm ribbon. Worked in wider ribbon, as in the yellow 7mm example, the stitch becomes bulky and unattractive.

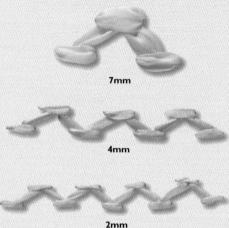

7mm

4mm

2mm

Method

Fig A Bring the needle up at **1**. Take it down at **2** and back through at **3**.

Fig B Take the needle down at **4** and back through at **5**.

Fig C Take the needle down at **6**. Bring the point back up, close to **4**, and pull the ribbon through.

Fig D Take the needle down at **7** and bring the point back up at **8**. Pull the ribbon through.

Fig E Take the needle down at **9** and bring it back up close to **7**.

Fig F Take the needle down at **10** and back through at **11**. Continue stitching in this way to end.

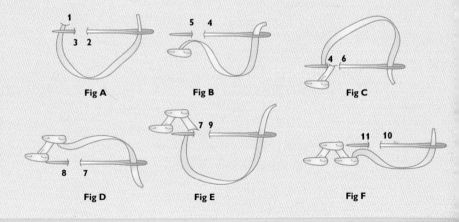

Fig A   Fig B   Fig C

Fig D   Fig E   Fig F

Fishbone Stitch

The decorative Fishbone Stitch may be used to create leaves or to form a woven border. It is effective when used to add contrast to designs that are fairly dense and solid in form. In the example, 13mm, 7mm, and 4mm ribbons have been used. For a more delicate effect, the stitch may be worked using 2mm ribbon.

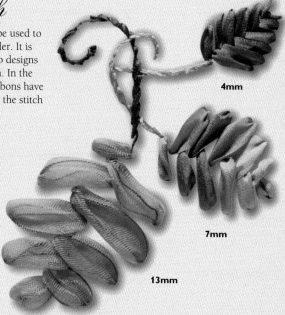

4mm

7mm

13mm

Method

Fig A Draw an outline of your design on the fabric. Bring the needle up at **1** and take it back down at **2**. The ribbon may be kept flat or allowed to twist.

Fig B Bring the needle up at **3** and down at **4**, crossing the base of the first stitch.

Fig C Bring the needle up at **5**.

Fig D Take the needle back down at **6**.

Fig E Bring the needle up at **7** and down at **8**. Continue in this way, working the stitches alternately on each side.

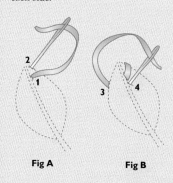

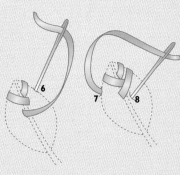

Fig A   Fig B   Fig C   Fig D   Fig E

Herringbone Stitch

Herringbone Stitch has numerous uses. It can
be worked as a border, or laced with contrasting
ribbon for a more decorative effect. It is also
used as a filler stitch, as for the basket in the
example. It is best worked in 2mm and 4mm
ribbon, and its height and width may be varied.
As with Chevron Stitch (*see page 80*), stitch
quality may suffer if wider ribbon is used.

4mm

2mm

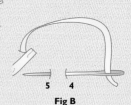

Fig A　　　　　　　　**Fig B**

Fig C

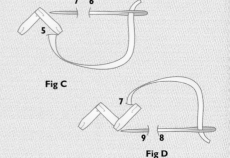

Fig D

Method

Fig A Bring the needle up at **1**. Take it down
at **2** and bring it back through at **3**. Try to
keep the ribbon flat.

Fig B Take the needle down at **4** and back
through at **5**.

Fig C Take the needle down at **6** and back
through at **7**.

Fig D Take the needle down at **8** and back
through at **9**. Continue in this way until the
design is complete.

Note Illustrated as ∧∨ in Motif Library.

Open Chain Stitch

Open Chain Stitch is one of many variations in the chain stitch family. It is often used to define other stitches in a design. In ribbon embroidery, it may be used as a foundation or filler stitch. It may be worked in varying widths of ribbon, and in any direction. Draw a stitch guide on the fabric before you begin.

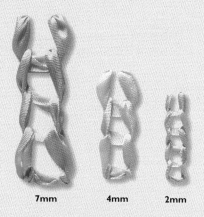

7mm   4mm   2mm

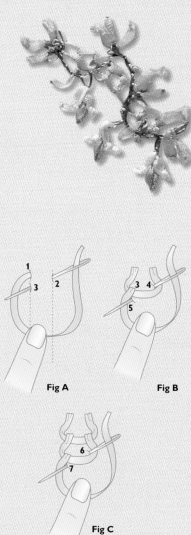

Fig A   Fig B

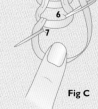

Fig C

Method

Fig A Bring the ribbon up at **1**. Take it down at **2** and bring it back up at **3**, noting the angle of the needle. The point of the needle must lie over the ribbon as shown.

Fig B Holding the ribbon down with your thumb, take the needle back down at **4** and bring it up at **5**. Pull the ribbon through.

Fig C Holding the ribbon flat, take the needle down at **6** and bring it back up at **7**. Work in the same way to the end. Fasten the ribbon at the back of the work.

Note Open Chain Stitch is also known as square stitch or ladder chain stitch.

Satin Stitch

In ribbon embroidery, Satin Stitch is often used with other stitches. It may be used as an infill stitch, or as the basis of an object such as the fish shown right. Before working a design it is advisable to draw it on the fabric, to ensure that the completed design has a smooth outline. The stitch may be worked using ribbons in a variety of widths, or in stranded threads, but for a delicate effect, it is best to use ribbon no more than 4mm wide. Satin Stitch may be worked horizontally, vertically, or at an angle.

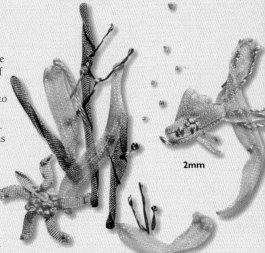

2mm

Method

Fig A Draw an outline of the design to be stitched. Fasten the ribbon to the back of the fabric. Bring the needle up at **1** and take it down at **2**.

Fig B Bring the ribbon up at **3**, close to **2**. Take it back down at **4**, keeping it flat and untwisted. The width of the stitch will be determined by the width of the ribbon. The Satin Stitch edges touch, filling in the design. Continue to stitch to the end.

Fig C The completed image. Fasten the ribbon to the back of the fabric.

Fig D The body of the fish shown above was worked in Satin Stitch. Straight Stitches (*see page 58*) were used for the fins and tail.

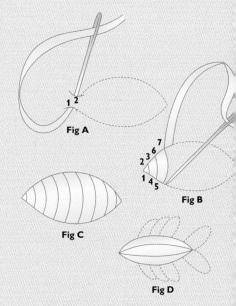

Fig A

Fig B

Fig C

Fig D

Note Illustrated as in Motif Library.
Uses Satin Stitch provides smooth, solid filling for areas in a design. It could be used to fill in fruit shapes, the sail of a boat, garments on a teddy bear or doll, a picture frame, or glass in a window.

Couching

The Couching technique uses a second needle and thread to attach a ribbon or embroidery thread to a design. A variety of stitches may be used to couch ribbon to fabric, as seen in this simple example. In ribbon embroidery, couching is often used to create the trailing ends of a bow. The ribbon may be couched flat, or folded and twisted to give the impression of movement. For other suitable couching stitches, see *Additional Embroidery Stitches*, page 129.

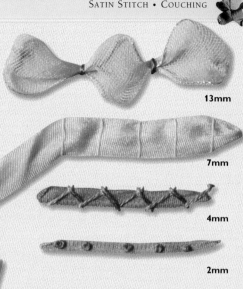

13mm

7mm

4mm

2mm

Method

Fig A Draw the outline of the design lightly on the fabric as a stitch guide. Fasten the ribbon to be couched at the back of the fabric and bring it up through the fabric at **1**. Lay it flat along the outline of the design and hold in place with your thumb.

Fig B Thread another needle with the couching thread. Bring the needle up to the left of **1** and take it across the ribbon. Take it down at **2** to form a small Straight Stitch (*see page 58*).

Fig C Bring the couching thread up at **3** and take it down at **4**. The space between couching stitches will be determined by the effect you wish to achieve.

Fig D Couch the ribbon to the end of the design line, then take the ribbon to the wrong side of the fabric. Fasten off. Take the couching thread to the wrong side of the fabric and fasten off.

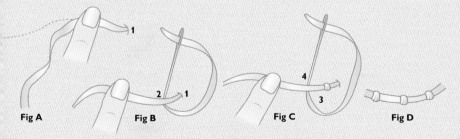

Fig A   Fig B   Fig C   Fig D

Note Illustrated as ▬▬▬ in Motif Library.
Uses Couched ribbon can be made into a bow to decorate a child's dress or christening robe. It may be used to frame a design, or to outline a motif filled in with decorative ribbon stitches. Use it as a border to trim a table runner or cushions.

Star Stitch

Star Stitch belongs to the cross stitch family. In ribbon embroidery, it is used as a decorative stitch. It may be worked singly, in lines or regular patterns, or sprinkled across an area as a filler stitch. Star Stitch may also be used as a basis for floral designs. Ribbon of various widths may be used, but 2mm and 4mm are most suitable. Before you begin, draw a stitch guide on the fabric.

| 2mm | 4mm | 7mm | 13mm |

Method

Fig A Draw a stitch guide on the fabric.

Fig B Bring the ribbon up at **1** and take it down at **2**. Bring it up at **3** and take it down at **4** to make a Cross Stitch. Bring the ribbon up again at **5**.

Fig C Take it down at **6**. Bring it up at **7** and take it down at **8** to make an Upright Cross Stitch. Fasten the ribbon at the back of the fabric.

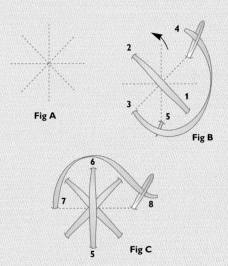

Fig A

Fig B

Fig C

Note Star Stitch is also known as Double Cross Stitch or Devil Stitch. Illustrated as ✳ in Motif Library.

Upright Cross Stitch

Upright Cross Stitch may be used as a foundation, filling, or border stitch in ribbon embroidery. Stitches may be worked singly, scattered, or as a solid pattern. It is best worked in 2mm and 4mm ribbons. Wider ribbon will look bulky and unattractive, unless the design is particularly large. To maintain even gauge, it is important to keep the ribbon flat and work the top stitches of each cross in the same direction.

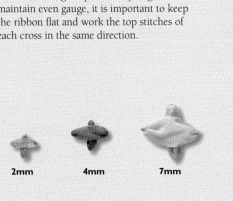

2mm **4mm** **7mm**

Method

Fig A Mark a stitch guide on the fabric. Work a line of evenly spaced running stitches from right to left: Bring the needle up at **1**. Take it down at **2** and then continue to end. Fasten the ribbon at the back.

Fig B Bring the ribbon up at **3**. Working from left to right, take it down at **4** to form a small Straight Stitch. Repeat the sequence to the end. Fasten the ribbon at the back of the work.

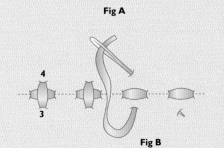

Fig A

Fig B

Notes For plain cross stitch, the foundation row is worked diagonally in one direction, then the top stitches are worked back diagonally in the opposite direction. To maintain even gauge on the ribbon, always work the top threads in the same direction, either from top to bottom or from bottom to top.

Rosette Chain Stitch

Rosette Chain Stitch may be worked in
embroidery thread, or in 2mm or 4mm
ribbon. It is a complicated and fairly dense
stitch that can look rather bulky if worked in
wider ribbon. It may be used as a border,
worked as a single stitch to create a rosette,
or used to make circular decorative shapes.
To ensure even gauge, some time and
care must be taken.

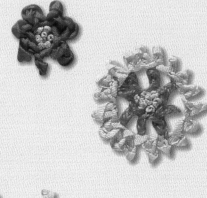

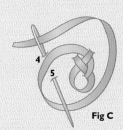

13mm   **7mm**   **4mm**   **2mm**

Method

Fig A Bring the ribbon up at **1**. Take the needle
down at an angle at **2** and up at **3**. Pass the
point of the needle over the ribbon as it is
brought up.

Fig B Pass the needle under the ribbon at **1**,
taking care not to pierce the fabric. Pull the
ribbon through. If working a rosette, take the

ribbon back down, close to **2**, and fasten it at
the back of the fabric.

Fig C To create a chain, take the needle down
at **4** and back up at **5**. Continue to the end,
working the steps as shown in Figures B and C.
Fasten the ribbon at the back.

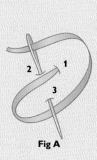

Fig A

Fig B

Fig C

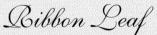

Ribbon Leaf

Many different stitches are used to create leaves. This Ribbon Leaf (seen in the example right) is partially detached, and is worked using fine thread that matches the color of the ribbon. This stitch was used frequently during the early Victorian period in decorative ribbon embroidery, both for soft furnishings, and for women's clothing. It may be made using ribbons in a variety of widths and in any direction.

13mm **7mm** **4mm** **2mm**

Method

Fig A Cut a piece of ribbon, twice the length of the desired leaf, plus ¼ in. (5mm) so it can be held between finger and thumb. Fold it in half. Thread a needle with matching thread and use a gathering stitch to sew the ribbon ends together close to the raw edge.

Fig B Pull the gathering stitches up and wind the thread around the base three times to fasten. Knot off the twists, but do not cut the thread.

Fig C Stitch the base of the leaf to the fabric. Bring the needle up at **1**. Take the needle through one side of the fold of the leaf at **2**. Then insert the needle back into the fabric at the base of the leaf at **3**. Pull the thread until the ribbon forms a leaf shape.

Fig D Curl the other side of the fold of the leaf into position as desired and stitch in place at **4**. The base will be covered with additional flowers or leaves.

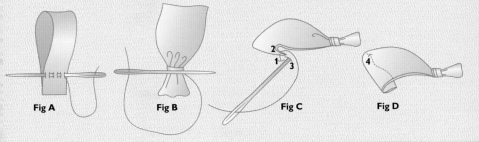

Fig A   Fig B   Fig C   Fig D

Gathered Ribbon Leaf

Gathered Ribbon Leaf is
worked with two needles.
It may be worked in any
direction, in a variety of
different widths of ribbon,
but narrow ribbon can be a
little difficult to handle. In
the example here, the anchor
stitches can be seen. In an
actual design, anchor stitches
are usually worked using
matching or invisible thread.

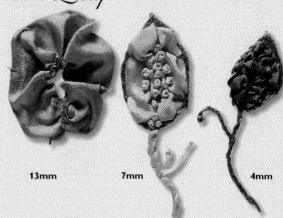

13mm   7mm   4mm

Method

Fig A Bring the ribbon to the surface of the
fabric at **1**. Using a fine crewel needle and one
strand of matching thread, work gathering
stitches through the center of the ribbon for
at least 2¼–2¾ in. (6–7cm)—further if using
wider ribbon. Slide the needle off the gathering
thread. Take the needle threaded with ribbon
back down into the fabric at **2**, leaving the
gathered loop above the surface. Fasten the
ribbon at the back of the fabric.

Fig B Pull the gathering stitches carefully until
the desired size is achieved. Knot the gathering
thread at the back of the fabric. Work tiny,
invisible stitches around the edges of the leaf to
anchor it to the fabric.

Fig C If you wish, you can fill the center of the
leaf with French Knots (*see page 70*).

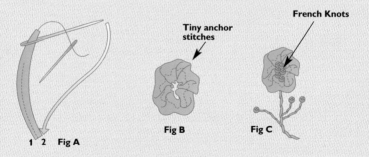

Tiny anchor
stitches

French Knots

1 2   Fig A

Fig B

Fig C

Note Illustrated as 〰 in Motif Library.

Flower Bud

This simple, yet effective, way to create buds is an ideal flower stitch for a beginner. Buds may be worked using ribbon in a variety of widths and in a range of sizes. For the example shown, Detached Chain Stitch (*see page 65*) was combined with Straight Stitch (*see page 58*).

13mm	7mm	4mm	2mm

Method

Fig A Bring the ribbon up at **1**. Form a loop and take the needle down at **2**. Bring the needle back up at **3**. Place a spare needle close to the exit point at **4**. Pass the ribbon over the spare needle and take it back down at **4**, noting that that the stitch is worked on a slant. Remove the spare needle and fasten the ribbon at the back of the fabric.

Fig B Using contrasting ribbon, bring the needle up at **5**. Take it back down at **6** to form a Straight Stitch. Bring it back up at **7** and take it down at **8**. Fasten the ribbon at the back of the fabric.

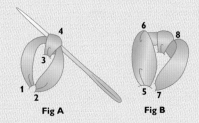

Fig A   Fig B

Note Other stitches suitable for flower buds include Ribbon Stitch (*see page 63*), Colonial Knot (*see page 69*), French Knot (*see page 70*), Bullion Knot (*see page 132*), and Twisted Detached Chain Stitch (*see page 66*).

Gathered Ribbon Flower

A variety of flowers can be created using this simple gathering technique. Experiment with different widths of ribbons for a more natural effect or try gathering more than one ribbon together at the same time. Note that 2mm ribbon is not wide enough for this technique to be effective. In this sample, the large flower has been worked by gathering white 13mm ribbon together with red 7mm ribbon. The smaller flower is made with white 7mm and red 4mm ribbons.

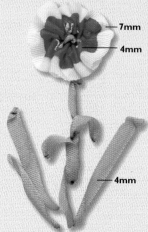

7mm
4mm
4mm

Method

Fig A Measure off a 4½ in. (11cm) length of ribbon. Using a needle threaded with matching thread, stitch tiny gathering stitches along one edge of the ribbon. (If working with more than one layer of ribbon, pin them together before stitching.)

Fig B Pull the ribbon up until it forms a neat circle. Tucking the raw edges to the back, stitch the two ends of the ribbon together. Stitch the flower into position on the fabric using matching thread.

13mm and 7mm

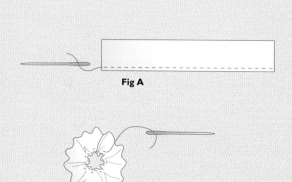

Fig A

Fig B

7mm and 4mm

Note Stamens can be added to the center of the flower, see page 95 for suggested stitches. Illustrated as ● in Motif Library.

Scrunched Gathered Flower

Making a Scrunched Gathered Flower is a very easy technique to master and an ideal way to use up short scraps of ribbon left over from other projects. Any width of ribbon may be used. Try layering ribbons on top of each other and gathering them together as one to create a multicolored, textured effect.

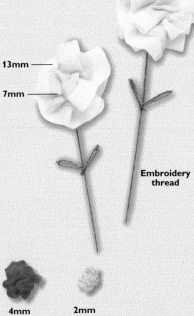

13mm —

7mm —

Embroidery thread

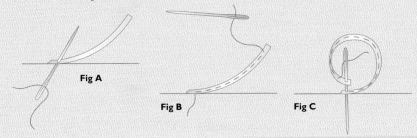

13mm   7mm   4mm   2mm

Method

Fig A Cut a length of ribbon approximately 2 in. (5cm) long. Bring a needle and matching thread up through the fabric and into one end of the ribbon.

Fig B Work small gathering stitches through the center of the length of ribbon.

Fig C Take the needle and thread back into the ribbon and fabric at the same entry point, ensuring that the ribbon ends sit on top of each other. Pull the thread through so that the ribbon gathers tightly. Fasten the thread at the back of the fabric.

Fig A

Fig B

Fig C

Note Illustrated as ● in Motif Library.

Stem Stitch

Stem Stitch is a versatile stitch with a wide variety of applications in many types of embroidery. It may be worked using ribbon of various widths, flat or twisted. Stitch length is determined by ribbon width, but very wide ribbons may make the stitch difficult to control. To ensure an attractive, even stitch, beginners should practice with 2mm, 4mm, and 7mm ribbon.

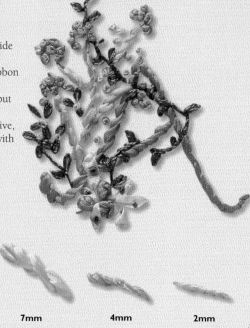

13mm **7mm** **4mm** **2mm**

Method

Fig A Draw a line on the fabric as a stitch guide. Bring the ribbon up at **1** and hold it out of the way with your thumb. Take it down at **2**, and bring it up at **3**.

Fig B Hold the ribbon out of the way with your thumb. Take the needle down at **4** and bring it back through at **5**, just to the right of **2**.

Fig C Work to the end of the design line. Fasten the ribbon at the back.

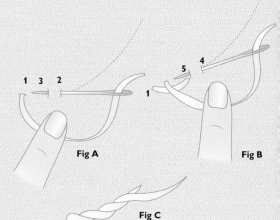

Fig A

Fig B

Fig C

Note Illustrated as ▬▬▬ in Motif Library.
Uses Stem Stitch is often used for vines, stems, borders, and lettering.

Stamens

Stamens are used to define a flower or plant. Suitable stitches include Straight Stitch (*see page 58*), Looped Straight Stitch (*see page 59*), Ribbon Filler Stitch (*see page 68*), Colonial Knot (*see page 69*), French Knot and extended French Knot (*see page 70*), and Bullion Knot (*see page 132*). For stamens similar to those in the examples here, use one or two strands of embroidery thread, or 2mm or 4mm ribbon. For very large designs, wider ribbon may be used, but care must be taken to maintain the proportions of the flower design.

Fig A Straight Stitch and French Knots
Fig B Extended twisted French Knots
Fig C Two examples of Looped Straight Stitch
Fig D Bullion Knot
Fig E Colonial Knot
Fig F Straight Stitch

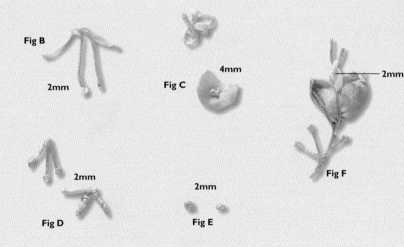

4mm

Fig A

Fig B

2mm

4mm

Fig C

2mm

2mm

Fig F

2mm

Fig D

2mm

Fig E

Pansy

This is one of the easiest ways to make a Pansy. It is ideal for a beginner to master before learning further gathering techniques. Ribbon flowers are often made separately, using gathering techniques. They are then appliquéd to the design, using small invisible stitches either through the center of the flower or through the petals. Use contrasting or dyed ribbons to create more realistic designs. Wider widths of ribbon are easier to work with.

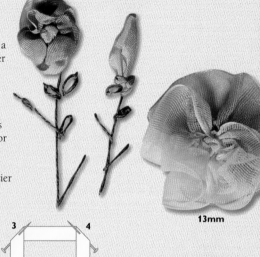

13mm

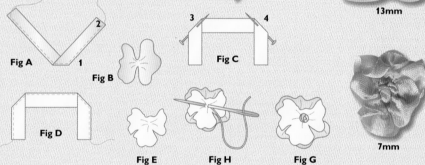

Fig A   Fig B   Fig C   Fig D   Fig E   Fig H   Fig G

7mm

Method

Fig A Cut a piece of ribbon approximately 3 in. (7cm) long. Fold it into a "V" shape, and pin the fold at **1**. Using a needle and matching thread and beginning at **2**, work a row of gathering stitches.

Fig B Pull the threads up tightly to form the base petal. Fasten off by stitching the ends of the ribbon together.

Fig C Cut another length of ribbon approximately 3½ in. (9cm) long. Fold it into thirds. Pin the folds at **3** and **4**.

Fig D Using a needle and matching thread, work a row of gathering stitches as shown.

Fig E Pull the stitches up tightly. Sew the ends together securely to form the under-petals.

Fig F Place the petal made in Fig B under the petal made in Fig E. Stitch them together. Attach the petals to the fabric using small, invisible stitches.

Fig G Add an extended French Knot (*see page 70*) or a Colonial Knot (*see page 69*) to the center using contrasting stranded thread or narrow ribbon.

Snowdrop

Snowdrops are extremely delicate flowers. Worked singly, they are ideal for bathroom and table linen, or for a child's garment. The petals are worked using Ribbon Stitch (*see page 63*). Twisted Straight Stitch (*see page 60*) is also suitable. For the example here, the flowers were worked in 2mm and 4mm ribbon. Wider ribbon may be used, but it is important to keep the dimensions of the design balanced. The petals are decorated with French Knots (*see page 70*) worked using two strands of embroidery thread. Stems and leaf stalks are worked in Straight Stitch (*see page 58*).

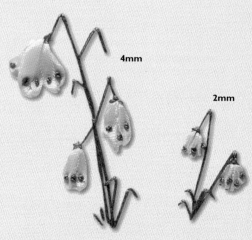

Method

Fig A Bring the ribbon up at **1**. Work a Ribbon Stitch to the left and take it down at **2**.

Fig B Bring the needle up, as close as possible to **1**, and work another Ribbon Stitch at **3**. Bring the needle up close to **1** again and take it down at **4**. Secure the ribbon at the back.

Fig C Complete the flower using two strands of embroidery thread. Work French Knots on the petals. Work the stem and leaf stalks in Straight Stitch.

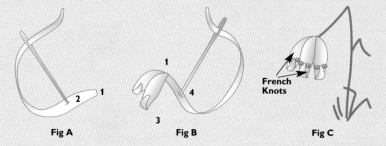

Fig A   Fig B   Fig C

Uses Snowdrops may also be used as "filler flowers" when an additional motif that will not dominate the overall design is needed.

Primrose

This basic Primrose design can be embellished with different stitches to create different flowers. Like ribbon embroidery rose variations (*see pages 109–114*), it is one of the most popular and most frequently worked flowers in ribbon embroidery. The five petals of a traditional Primrose are worked in Straight Stitch (*see page 58*), from the center out to each point as in the example here. When using 7mm, 13mm, or wider ribbon, the petals may be worked over a chopstick to add height. Use a spare needle to control the entry and exit points of the stitch. A single French Knot (*see page 70*) forms the flower center.

| 13mm | 7mm | 4mm | 2mm |

Method
Fig A Bring the needle up at **1**. Keeping the ribbon flat, make a Straight Stitch at **2**.

Fig B Create five Straight Stitch petals, working each stitch from the center of the design.

Fig C Using contrasting ribbon, work a French Knot in the center of the flower.

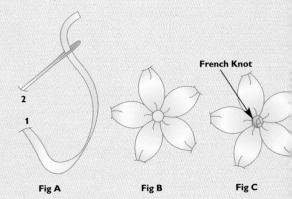

French Knot

Fig A   **Fig B**   **Fig C**

Closed Iris

A variety of flowers are created using Detached Chain Stitch (*see page 65*). A Closed Iris combines Detached Chain Stitch with Straight Stitch (*see page 58*) and Twisted Straight Stitch (*see page 60*). Before you begin, it is important to mark the center, height, and width of the flower on the fabric to guide your stitches and ensure continuity of design.

13mm   7mm   4mm   2mm

Method

Fig A Mark the stitch guide on the fabric.

Fig B Work a single Detached Chain Stitch.

Fig C Bring the ribbon up at **1** and pass the needle under the base of the chain. Take the needle back down at **2**. Do not pull the stitch tight. Fasten at the back of fabric.

Fig D For the stem, bring the needle up at the base of the chain, and make one long Twisted Straight Stitch at **3**, allowing the ribbon to twist just once. Fasten at the back.

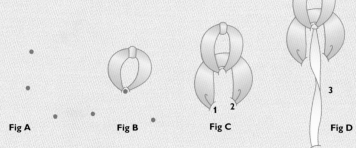

Fig A   Fig B   Fig C   Fig D

Note Illustrated as 🎀 in Motif Library.

Lily

Lilies were once a symbol of death, but today they are often seen as a flower of celebration and used in bridal bouquets and other decorative floral displays. They may be worked in any width of ribbon. Alone, or in a bouquet, they always look stunning. For the example here, the head was worked in Ribbon Stitch (*see page 63*), and a Bullion Knot (*see page 132*) added for the center. Stems may be worked in ribbon or embroidery thread. Suitable stitches include Twisted Stem Stitch (*see page 94*) and Whipped Running Stitch (*see page 73*).

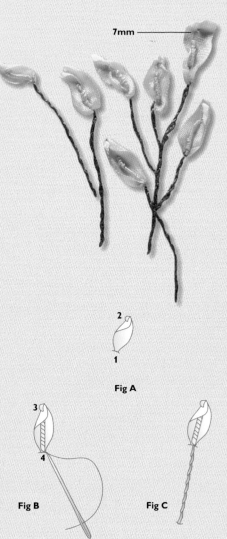

7mm

Method

Fig A Bring the ribbon to the surface of the fabric at **1**. Make a Ribbon Stitch with the ribbon curl at the tip (**2**) either to the right or left. Fasten the ribbon at the back of the fabric.

Fig B Bring a needle, threaded with either embroidery thread or 2mm silk ribbon, up through the fabric and ribbon beneath the tip of the lily head at **3**. Make a Bullion Knot (*see page 127*) with six or more wraps. Take the needle down at **4**, maintaining a firm tension on the wraps. Fasten the stitch at back.

Fig C Work a stem using one of the suggested stitches. Stem Stitch (*see page 94*) was used for the example above.

Fig A

Fig B

Fig C

Notes In freestyle embroidery, the lily heads may be worked in stiffened silk ribbon and attached to wired stems. This technique is particularly effective for three-dimensional work.

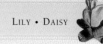

Daisy

Ribbon of any width may be used
to create Daisies. Petals are worked
in Ribbon Stitch (*see page 63*) and
may be worked in any direction.
French Knots (*see page 70*) form
the center. It is advisable to draw a
daisy outline on the fabric as a stitch
guide. Use Stem Stitch (*see page 94*)
or Twisted Straight Stitch (*see page
60*) for the stems.

7mm

4mm

4mm

7mm

4mm

7mm

Method

Fig A Draw a stitch guide on the fabric.
Working from the center of the flower, bring
the needle up at **1**. Work a Ribbon Stitch and
take the needle down at **2**. Bring the needle
back up at **3** and take it down at **4**. Continue to
work petals in this way.

Fig B Using 2mm ribbon to create French
Knots, complete the center of the flower. Work
the stem and leaves in Twisted Straight Stitch.

Fig C For an alternative drooping daisy, draw a
stitch guide on the fabric. Work the petals in a
downward direction, using Ribbon Stitch.
Work the flower center in French Knots and
the stem in Stem Stitch. Work the leaves
in a decorative stitch such as Cretan
Stitch (*see page 78*).

Fig A

Fig B

Fig C

Note Experiment with decorative stitches such
as Cretan Stitch (*see page 78*) or Chained
Feather Stitch (*see page 76*) to create interesting
leaf shapes.

Ivy

Ivy is often used in ribbon embroidery to
decorate floral designs and garden scenes.
It is very easy to work and may be made
in any direction, using any width of
ribbon. Stems may be worked in ribbon
or embroidery thread. Stem Stitch (*see
page 94*) was used for the example here.
The ivy was worked using Ribbon Stitch
(*see page 63*).

2mm

4mm

7mm

13mm

Method

Fig A Draw a stitch guide for the stem on the
fabric. Work in Stem Stitch.

Fig B Bring the ribbon up close to the end of
the stem. Work three Ribbon Stitches in the
sequence suggested, making the center stitch at
3 slightly longer than the side stitches **1** and **2**.
When the center section of the leaf is complete,
take the needle to the back of the fabric and
fasten the ribbon.

Fig A

Fig B

1

2

3

Note The ivy may be stitched in different widths
and tones of ribbon, for example 2mm, 4mm, and
7mm, to indicate new and mature foliage.

Holly

Holly leaves are another example of gathered stitch worked using two needles. Work a loose Straight Stitch (*see page 58*) to form a ribbon loop. Gather this loop using a second needle and matching thread. Attach the leaf to the fabric using tiny Straight Stitches that represent the points or thorns. Add French Knots (*see page 70*) or tiny beads to represent berries. For each leaf, you will need ribbon twice the length of the finished leaf.

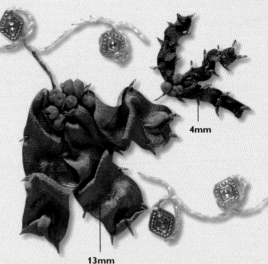

4mm

13mm

Method

Fig A Draw the holly leaf design on the fabric. Note the working order for stitching.

Fig B Bring the ribbon up at **1** and take it down at **2** to form a loose Straight Stitch. Fasten at the back of the work. Repeat, following the suggested order, until three loose Straight Stitches have been made.

Fig C Thread a crewel needle with matching thread and bring it up at **1**. Make tiny gathering stitches through the center of the first Straight Stitch. Pull up to gather the ribbon. Take the

needle down at **2** and fasten the thread at the back. Repeat this process for each leaf.

Fig D Work tiny Straight Stitches around each leaf.

Fig E For the berries, work French Knots or attach small beads close to the base of the leaf.

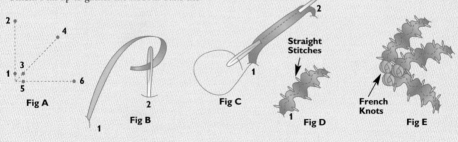

Fig A

Fig B

Fig C
Straight
Stitches

Fig D

Fig E
French
Knots

Pine Cone

Pine Cones may be made using different widths of ribbon. The stitch used will often determine the width. If the stitch is fairly dense, narrow ribbon will give the design a neater and more even finish. The ribbon may be kept flat or allowed to twist. The woven stitch used to form the pine cones here requires a little practice and patience. Fishbone Stitch (*see page 81*) and Cretan Stitch (*see page 78*) are also suitable.

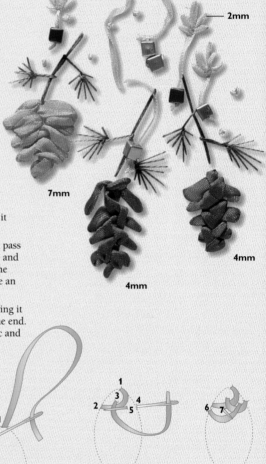

4mm

2mm

7mm

4mm

4mm

Method

Fig A Draw the outline of the design on the fabric.

Fig B Bring the ribbon up at **1** and take it down at **2**.

Fig C Bring the needle back up at **3** and pass it over the first stitch. Take it down at **4** and back up at **5**, weaving the needle over the ribbon. Pull the ribbon gently to achieve an even gauge.

Fig D Take the needle down at **6** and bring it up at **7**. Repeat steps **4**, **5**, **6**, and **7** to the end. Take the ribbon to the back of the fabric and fasten off.

Fig A

Fig B

Fig C

Fig D

Notes Use beads to embellish the design. Attach a bead to one end of narrow ribbon and stitch the other end to the fabric, leaving the beaded end free. This motif is ideal for holiday cards.

Basic Fuchsia

This Basic Fuchsia may be developed to form more complicated blooms. Lower petals are worked in Straight Stitch (*see page 58*), and upper petals in Looped Straight Stitch (*see page 59*). Ribbon Stitch forms the upper sepals (*see page 63*), and the sepals are worked using extended French Knots (*see page 70*) and two strands of embroidery thread.

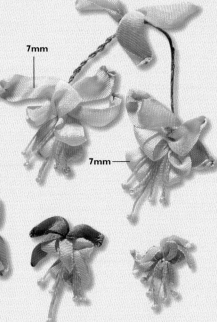

7mm

7mm

13mm   7mm   4mm   2mm

Method

Fig A Draw the lower three petal shapes on the fabric and embroider Straight Stitch petals. Work the petals at **1** and **2** first, then the center petal **3**, letting it overlap the outer petals.

Fig B Work three Looped Straight Stitches above the base petals at **4**, **5**, and **6**. Work downward, following the suggested order. Tease the loops out with a spare needle.

Fig C Using a contrasting ribbon and Ribbon Stitch, work three sepals at **7**, **8**, and **9**, following the stitch guide. Keep the stitches as close as possible to the entry point of the upper petals, and allow the ribbon to twist.

Fig D Using extended French Knots and two strands of embroidery thread, work several stigmas. The stitches sit between the folds of the lower and upper petals at **10**. Add stems and more leaves as desired.

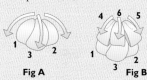

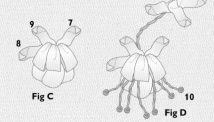

Fig A   Fig B   Fig C   Fig D

Notes Stigmas may be made using Straight Stitch and finished with tiny glass beads. For more creative ideas, consult gardening and botanical reference books.

Chinese Lantern

The Chinese Lantern is a simple and effective flower design. Ribbon Stitch (*see page 63*) is used for the leaves, so it is an excellent way to practice using two needles. The flower heads may be worked using ribbon in a variety of widths. It is important to remember that the petals are worked in a downward direction. Stems are worked using Straight Stitch (*see page 58*) and stranded embroidery thread.

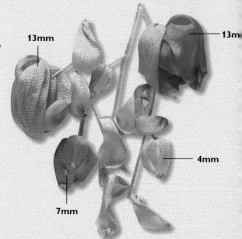

Method

Fig A Bring the ribbon to the surface of the fabric at **1**. Place a second needle under the ribbon. Take the needle down through the ribbon at **2**. Gently lift the finished stitch with the second needle so that it is soft and rounded.

Fig B Work the two outer petals in the same way, making sure they overlap the base petal. Take the ribbon to the back and secure. Work the stem using one or two strands of embroidery thread. Work the leaves in Ribbon Stitch.

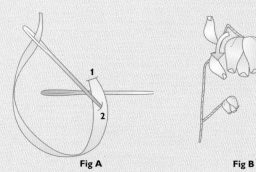

Fig A

Fig B

Notes Stitch buds using narrower ribbon. For a more natural effect, try variegated dyed silk ribbon. For a more three-dimensional effect, a Padded Rosebud (*see page 110*) may be substituted.

Bleeding Heart

The popular Bleeding Heart may be worked in a variety of ribbon widths. It is worked in a downward direction. Outer petals are Couched (*see page 85*) in place using a small Straight Stitch. The delicate center of the flower is an extended Detached Chain Stitch (*see page 65*). Stems may be Couched or worked in Stem Stitch (*see page 94*). Beginners should mark a stitch guide on the fabric to ensure correct dimensions for the flowers.

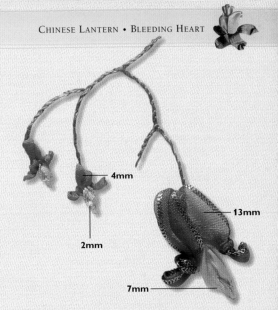

4mm

13mm

2mm

7mm

Method

Fig A Bring the ribbon up at **1** and take it down at **2**. Do not pull it taut as it should form a soft loop.

Fig B Bring the needle up at **3** and pass it over the original stitch. Take it back down at **4**, securing the first loop to the fabric. Fasten the ribbon at the back.

Fig C Bring the ribbon up at **5** and take down at **6**, again forming a soft loop. Bring the needle up again at **7** and take it back down at **8**. Fasten the ribbon at the back.

Fig D The completed outer petals.

Fig E Using contrasting ribbon, work an extended Detached Chain Stitch at the base of the outer petals.

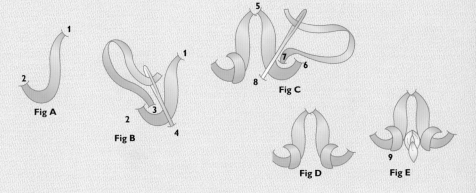

Fig A

Fig B

Fig C

Fig D

Fig E

Note Illustrated as ![motif] in Motif Library.

Cattail

The Cattail is a versatile image suitable for floral, water, and country designs. In this example, 4mm ribbon was used for the head and leaves, and embroidery thread for the stems and tip. Create the head by working a row of tiny stitches through the center of the ribbon, then pulling gently to gather them. Twisted Straight Stitch (*see page 60*) forms the leaves.

Method

Fig A Bring the ribbon up at **1**. Take a second needle and one strand of embroidery thread and bring it up at the same entry point as the ribbon. Work tiny gathering stitches through the center of the ribbon for about 4 in. (10cm), then pull to gather.

Fig B Take both needles down at **2**. Fasten ribbon and embroidery thread at the back of the fabric.

Fig C With the needle and embroidery thread, make a small Straight Stitch at the top of the gathered ribbon at **2**. Fasten the thread at the back. Bring the same needle and thread up again close to **1**, and then take it back down at **3** to form a stalk. Fasten the thread at the back of the fabric.

Fig D Attach leaves to the stalk using Twisted Straight Stitch.

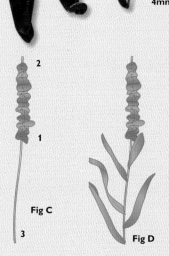

4mm

4mm

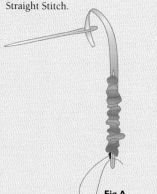

Fig A

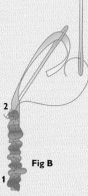

Fig B

Fig C

Fig D

Notes Vary the size of the cattail head by using ribbon in different widths and by gathering 6–8 in. (15–20cm) lengths instead of the 4 in. (10cm) lengths used in this example.

Rosebud

This Rosebud is a combination of Twisted Detached Chain Stitch (*see page 66*), Straight Stitch (*see page 58*), and Ribbon Stitch (*see page 63*). Finer details may be added to the rosebud using stranded embroidery thread. Try using Rosebuds with Folded Ribbon or Concertina Roses to create a beautiful floral garland. Ribbons in a variety of colors and widths may be used.

Method

Fig A Use two shades of ribbon to create the bud—one darker, one lighter. Fasten the darker ribbon to the back of the fabric. Bring it up to the surface at **1** and create a Twisted Detached Chain Stitch.

Fig B Fasten the lighter ribbon to the back of the fabric. Bring the needle up at **2**. Keeping the ribbon flat, make a Straight Stitch across the bud. Take the needle down at **3**.

Fig C Bring the needle up at **4** and take it back down at **5** and fasten it off. The Straight Stitches sit over the Detached Chain Stitch, leaving the point of the chain protruding.

Fig D Using ribbon in a color to indicate the sepals, work two Ribbon Stitches over the Straight Stitches at **6** and **7**. If desired, add details to the rosebud using stranded embroidery thread.

13mm

13mm

4mm

7mm

Fig A

1

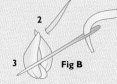

2

3   Fig B

4

5

Fig C

6   7

Fig D

Padded Rosebud

A Padded Rosebud is an effective way
to create three-dimensional images.
For the example here, Ribbon Stitch
(*see page 63*) was used to work the
petals and leaf, Grab Stitch (*see page
64*) for the calyx, and a single Straight
Stitch (*see page 58*) for the stem.
Other stitches may be combined to
produce padded flowers and objects;
experiment with a variety of stitches to
create your own designs. Any width
of ribbon may be used for a Padded
Rosebud. This example was worked
in 7mm ribbon.

7mm

Method

Fig A Using a fine needle and matching thread,
secure a bead to the fabric.

Fig B Thread a needle with ribbon. Bring the
ribbon up at **1**, work a Ribbon Stitch over the
bead and take the needle down at **2**. Control
the entry and exit points of the ribbon
using a spare needle.

Fig C Bring the needle up as close to **1** as
possible. Work a second Ribbon Stitch to the
right of the first at **3**. Overlap the stitches.
Work another Ribbon Stitch to the left of the
first at **4**, covering the bead completely.

Fig D Work another petal on the other side of
the bud at **5**.

Fig E Work two further Ribbon Stitch petals at
6 and **7**. Using the same length of ribbon and
Grab Stitch, work the calyx at **8**. Work the
stem in Straight Stitch at **9**. Work a single leaf
in Ribbon Stitch, extending from the middle
of the stem.

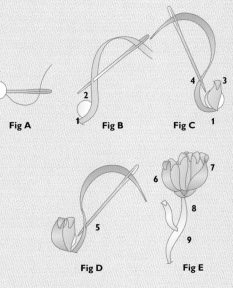

Notes The size and shape of the rosebud is
determined by the width of the ribbon and the
size of the bead used. Illustrated as 🌷 in
Motif Library.

Concertina Rose

Traditionally, simple decorations for festive events were made by folding strips of crèpe paper together in an overlapping technique. When the folds were released, they would form a "swag" of interwoven paper. A Concertina Rose is made by folding ribbon in a similar manner. Once the folds are released, the ends of the ribbon are pulled, forming a rose in the center.

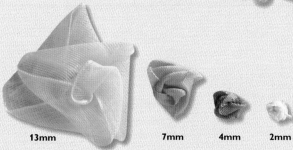

| 13mm | 7mm | 4mm | 2mm |

Method

Fig A Cut a 10 in. (25cm) length of ribbon. Fold it at right angles in the center. Hold in place. Bring the lower half of the ribbon up and over the fold, ensuring that the fold sits at the edge of the ribbon and remains at right angles. Hold the new fold in place. Again, bring the lower ribbon up and over the new fold.

Fig B Fold the ribbon several times more.

Fig C Hold the two ends of the ribbon firmly. Allow the folds to release. Pull carefully on one end of the ribbon, so the folds pull into the center to form a rose.

Fig D Pull the ribbon until you are happy with the shape. Hold the two ends together and bring a needle and thread up through the center of the rose and back through to the base.

Fig E Wrap the thread around to secure the base. Trim the excess ribbon leaving a ¼ in. (6mm) tail. Press the tail to one side. Attach the rose to the fabric using tiny stitches.

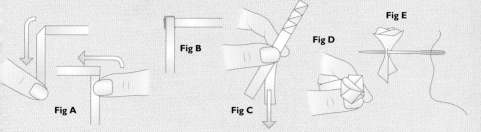

Fig A

Fig B

Fig C

Fig D

Fig E

Notes Roses may be made in a variety of ribbons including silk, chiffon, and satin, depending on the effect required. For a soft rose, use silk ribbon. For extra body, use double-sided satin ribbon. Roses may be worked singly or in groups.

Spider Web Rose

Spider Web Rose is a popular stitch also known as Spider Web Filling. It is based on a series of linked stitches, worked in a circular shape. The ribbon is woven under and over these stitches to form a flower shape.

13mm

Method

Fig A Thread a needle with one strand of embroidery thread in a color that matches the ribbon being used, and knot the end of the thread. Bring the thread to the surface of the fabric at **1**. Making a Straight Stitch to the right, take the needle down at **2** and back up at **3**. Work this first stitch fairly loosely. Pass the needle over the center of the first stitch and take it back down into the fabric at **4**.

Fig B Bring the needle up at **5** and take it back down at **3**.

Fig C Bring the needle back up at **6** and take it back down at **3**. Fasten the thread at the back of the fabric.

Fig D The completed base for the stitch.

Fig E Thread a needle with silk ribbon and fasten it at the back of the fabric. Bring the needle up in the center of the circular shape, near **3**. Take the needle under the first thread and over the next. Do not pierce the fabric.

Fig F Weave the ribbon under and over alternate stitches, allowing it to twist. Work with a relaxed gauge and tease out the petals with the point of the needle. When the flower is formed, and all the base embroidery thread stitches are covered, take the needle down to the wrong side of the fabric and fasten off the ribbon.

7mm

4mm

2mm

Fig A

Fig B

Fig C

Fig D

Needle
under
thread

Over
thread

Fig E

Fig F

Note Illustrated as 🌀 in Motif Library.
Uses Try using different shades of one color for a variegated effect.

Folded Ribbon Rose

As the name suggests, the Folded Ribbon Rose is made by folding ribbon, then attaching each fold to the base of the first few folds to create petals. Worked in wider ribbon, it is ideal for three-dimensional designs. Completed roses are attached to fabric using a needle and thread.

Fig A

Fig B`

Fig C

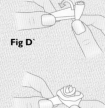

Fig D`

Fig E

Fig F

Method

Fig A   Cut a piece of ribbon approximately 10 in. (25cm) long. Hold it horizontally with your left hand and fold over the right end diagonally. Leave a tail of ribbon ¾ in. (1.5cm) long.

Fig B With your right hand, roll the diagonal fold toward the left. Roll it over three times to form the center of the rose.

Fig C Pinch the end of the base of the folds. Stitch through to hold them in place.

Fig D Hold the base of the rose with your right hand. Fold the ribbon back with your left hand. Wrap the folded ribbon once around the center of the rose. Stitch the fold to the base.

Fig E Fold the top edge of the ribbon back down. Wrap the folded ribbon once more around the center. Stitch the fold to the base. Continue to fold, wrap, and stitch, relaxing the gauge on the ribbon as you work the outer petals.

Fig F When the rose is the desired shape and size, stitch through the base to secure all the wraps and folds. Trim off the excess ribbon. Attach the finished rose to the fabric using small invisible stitches.

13mm

7mm

4mm

Twirled Ribbon Rose

A Twirled Ribbon Rose is very simple to make. A length of silk ribbon is twisted until it forms a soft cord, which is then stitched on to, and through, fabric. As the loops of ribbon are pulled through the fabric they form petals. This stitch requires only short lengths of ribbon, so it is an ideal way to use up scraps left over from other projects.

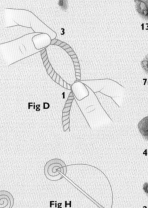

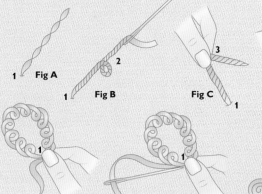

13mm

7mm

4mm

2mm

Method

Fig A Fasten the ribbon to the back of the fabric. Bring the needle up at **1**. Twist the ribbon in a counter-clockwise direction.

Fig B The ribbon will begin to kink, as seen at **2**.

Fig C Take hold of the twisted ribbon with your finger and thumb at **3**, approximately 1¼ in. (3cm) from the point of entry at **1**.

Fig D With your other hand, pinch the ribbon together close to **1** to form a twisted loop.

Fig E Still holding the ribbon together at **1**, release the top end of the loop. Allow the ribbon to loosely untwist, to form a soft cord.

Fig F Still holding the cord together at **1**, take the needle and the remaining ribbon back down to the wrong side of the fabric, as close as possible to **1**.

Fig G Gently pull the twisted ribbon through the fabric until the rose is formed. Fasten off the ribbon at the back of the fabric.

Fig H Fasten the rose to the fabric with matching embroidery thread, by stitching up through the center and back through to the wrong side of the fabric.

Note Illustrated as ● in Motif Library.
Uses This rose has very tightly coiled petals. It is ideal for garden scenes, where a climbing rose may be depicted with buds and roses in various stage of flower.

Parrot

This colorful Parrot takes a little practice but it is an attractive motif for kitchen linen or children's clothing. The bird's head is worked using Ribbon Stitch (*see page 63*). The body and wings are worked using overlapping Straight Stitches (*see page 58*) and ribbon in a variety of colors. For the example here, 2mm, 4mm, and 7mm ribbons were used.

Method

Fig A Using 7mm ribbon, bring the needle up at **1**. Work a Ribbon Stitch and take it down at **2**. Allow the ribbon to curl. Fasten the ribbon at the back.

Fig B Bring the ribbon up at **3** and work a Straight Stitch. Take it down at **4**. Do not make the stitch tight—it should sit softly on the fabric. Fasten the ribbon.

Fig C Bring the ribbon up at **5** and take it down at **6**. Fasten the ribbon.

Fig D Bring the ribbon up at **7**. Control the stitch over a second needle to create a soft, slightly raised stitch. Take it down at **8**. Fasten the ribbon.

Fig E Using 4mm ribbon in a contrasting color and following the stitch guide, highlight the bird using Straight Stitches, 4mm wide, at points **9**, **10**, **11**, **12**, and **13**. Using 2mm ribbon and following the stitch guide, work three overlapping tail feathers as at **14**.

Fig F Add a French Knot for the eye, and Straight Stitches for the beak and plume details using two strands of embroidery thread.

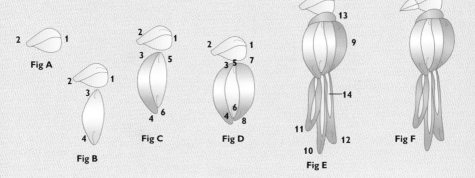

Fig A

Fig B

Fig C

Fig D

Fig E

Fig F

Dragonfly

Insects, birds, fish, and animals add interest to embroidered images, and can bring water- or nature-based scenes to life. Individually, they are useful motifs for greetings cards, scented herb pillows, fabric picture frames, and linen. The Dragonfly is a fragile insect and working it in 2mm and 4mm ribbon reflects its delicacy. The body and wings of the example here were worked using Straight Stitch (*see page 58*) and the eyes were worked in French Knots (*see page 70*).

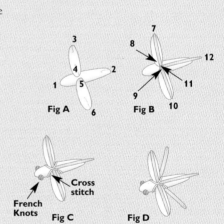

4mm

2mm

2mm

2mm

4mm

4mm

4mm

Method

Fig A Using 4mm ribbon, bring the needle up at **1**. Keeping the ribbon flat, work a Straight Stitch. Take the needle down at **2** and fasten the ribbon. Bring it up at **3** and work a Straight Stitch, piercing the original stitch at **4**. Take the ribbon to the back and fasten. Bring it up at **5**, piercing the original stitch. Take it down at **6** and fasten.

Fig B Using 2mm ribbon, bring the needle up at **7** and take it down at **8**. Bring it up at **9** and take it down at **10**. Fasten the ribbon. Bring it up at **11** and down at **12**. Fasten it at the back.

Fig C Using one or two strands of embroidery thread, work French Knots for the eyes and a small cross stitch where the wings join the body.

Fig D Add more wings if desired.

Fig A

Fig B

Fig C

Fig D

French Knots

Cross stitch

Notes Use silk organza ribbons for the wings to create a transparent effect. Make the eyes using tiny glass beads.

Sheep

Sheep are fun to create in ribbon. They may be embroidered on children's clothing or used on gift cards. French Knots (*see page 70*) or Colonial Knots (*see page 69*) are ideal for creating the wool. For larger Sheep, use wider ribbons and enlarge the template on a photocopier. In the example here, 2mm ribbon was used for the French Knots and the details were worked using two strands of embroidery thread.

2mm

Method

Fig A Using two strands of black embroidery thread and Satin Stitch (*see page 84*), work the head of the sheep. Fasten the thread at the back of the fabric.

Fig B Keeping the stitches close together, work the body of the sheep in either French Knots or Colonial Knots. Work a single French Knot for the eye.

Fig C Work the ears, tail, and legs using Straight Stitch (*see page 58*) and two strands of black embroidery thread.

Fig A

Fig B

Fig C

Fish

Underwater scenes are fun to create and Fish can be simple or intricate depending on your imagination and level of skill. The technique shown here is very simple to achieve. The body of the Fish is worked in Straight Stitch (*see page 58*), and details are worked using one or two strands of embroidery thread. For similar fish, use 2mm, 4mm, and 7mm ribbon. The size of the fish will be determined by the width of the ribbon.

Method

Fig A Bring the ribbon up at **1**, make a Straight Stitch and take it down at **2**. Fasten the ribbon at the back.

Fig B Bring the ribbon up at **3**, slightly in front of the entry point of the original stitch. Take it down close to **2**. Fasten the ribbon.

Fig C Bring the ribbon up at **4**. Pass the needle under the Straight Stitch, taking care not to pierce the fabric, and take it down at **5**. Fasten the ribbon.

Fig D Using one or two strands of embroidery thread and small Straight Stitches, work the upper fin and gills. Work the eyes and lips using French Knots (*see page 70*).

Fig E Work the lower fins in Straight Stitch or Stem Stitch (*see page 58 or 94*).

Notes For inspiration, look at books on fish and marine life. Beads and decorative threads may be used to create coral and seaweed.

Butterfly

Butterflies are easy and quick to make, and may be worked in any direction. They may be used singly, or incorporated in a floral design. Wings are made using Ribbon Stitch (*see page 63*) and the body is worked in Stem Stitch (*see page 94*) and Satin Stitch (*see page 84*). Extended French Knots (*see page 70*) decorate the wings. For the example here, 13mm ribbon was used. Use narrower or wider ribbon to create smaller or larger Butterflies. For more complex designs, experiment with decorative embroidery thread.

13mm

Method

Fig A Work three overlapping Ribbon Stitches in the order shown. Control the stitch entry and exit points using a spare needle. Fasten the ribbon at the back using a needle and thread. Work the body using Stem Stitch and two strands of embroidery thread. Work French Knots at the end of the antennae. Work the legs using Straight Stitch (*see page 58*).

Fig B For an alternative butterfly, work four wings using Ribbon Stitch as shown. Fasten the ribbon at the back of the work. Work the body as for Fig A. Embellish the wings with embroidery stitching and extended French Knots.

13mm

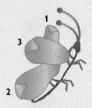

Fig A

Fig B

Note Small glass beads may be used to decorate the wings and body or to create eyes.

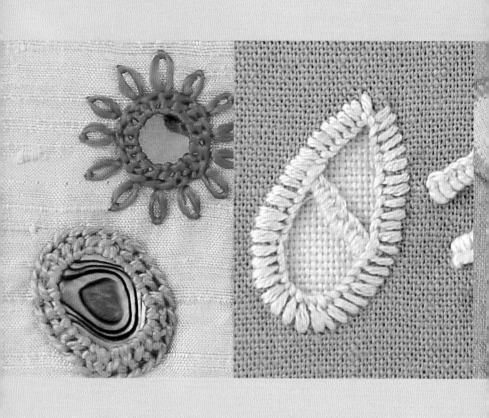

Additional Embroidery Stitches

The freestyle embroidery stitches in this section are just a few of the many used to enhance and support ribbon embroidery designs. Stitches may be used for details such as stamens, for delicate detail such as shadow work, and to suggest dimension. The key to the creation of original and signature work is experimentation with different stitches.

Chain Stitch and Whipped Chain Stitch

Lengths of Chain Stitch are often used for making stems and leaves to support ribbon flowers. Whipped Chain Stitch forms a more substantial stem. Both Chain and Whipped Chain Stitch may also be used for decorative borders and outlines.

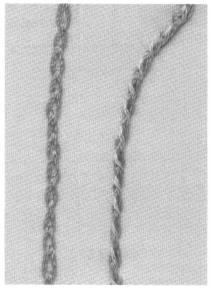

Work from top to bottom.

Fig A Bring needle up at **1** and insert at same place, forming a loop. Bring needle back up at **2**, looping the thread beneath needle as shown.

Fig B Insert needle in same place as **2**, inside loop of stitch above. Loop the thread beneath the needle as before and bring needle back up at **3**.

Fig C Repeat as required to form a linked chain. All stitches should be the same length.

Whipped Chain Stitch
Fig D Bring a needle with either matching or contrasting thread up as close to **1** as possible.

Fig E Without piercing the fabric, pass the needle under each Chain Stitch along the linked chain. To finish, fasten the thread at the back of the fabric.

Fig A

Fig B

Fig C   **Fig D**   **Fig E**

Note Illustrated as ◖◗◖◗ in Motif Library.

Buttonhole Stitch

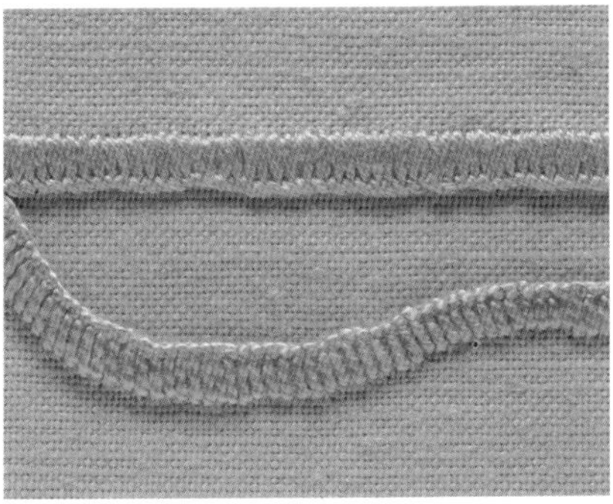

Buttonhole Stitch is worked in the same way as Blanket Stitch (*see page 134*), but with the stitches so close together that no fabric can be seen between them. The basic stitch seals and finishes the edges of fabric cut to make a buttonhole. Several decorative stitches belong to the buttonhole stitch family.

Working from left to right, the twisted edge forms at the lower line.

Work as for Blanket Stitch, but place the stitches very close together with no fabric showing between them. In cut work, unwanted fabric is always cut away close to the twisted lower edge, never from the upper edge.

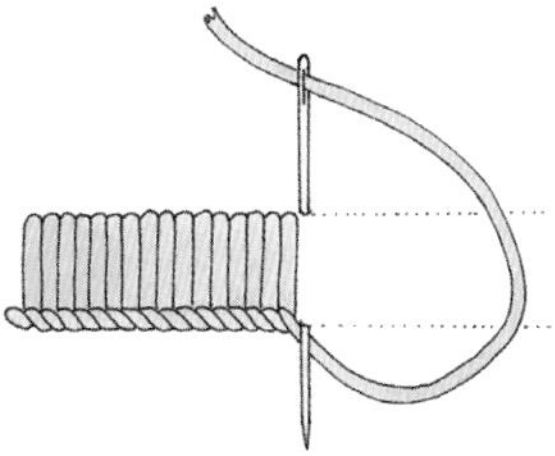

Buttonhole Bar

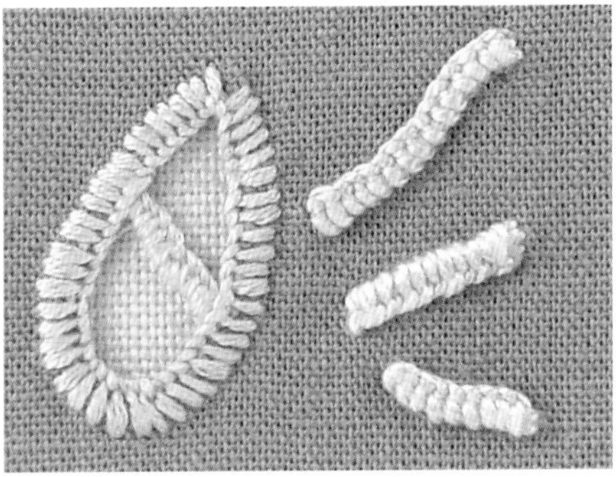

This versatile stitch from the buttonhole stitch family is used in many different forms of embroidery. Worked in fine embroidery threads, it is useful for stems and leaves. It is also good as a decorative outline, for flowers, or for insects such as a caterpillar.

Fig A Bring needle up at **1**, down at **2**, up a tiny distance away at **3**, and down at **4**. Bring needle out again just below **1** to begin Buttonhole Stitch.

Fig B Work Buttonhole Stitch from left to right over the two long stitches made, without piercing the fabric, packing stitches firmly so bar lies flat. At right end of bar, insert needle just below point **2** to fasten off last loop.

Fig A

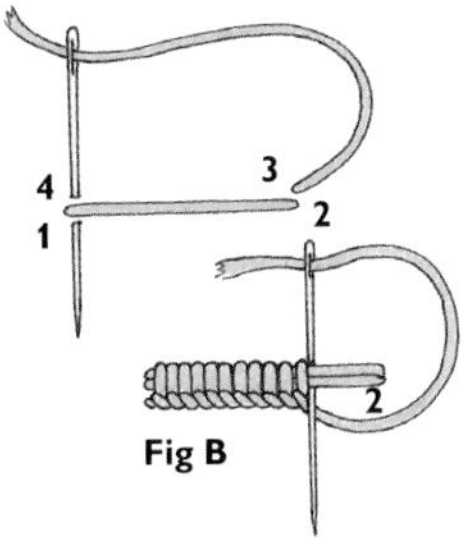

Fig B

Note Illustrated as in Motif Library.

Buttonhole Flowers and Wheels

For Buttonhole Flowers, the linked stitches are worked so they form a circle in the center and the straight part of the stitch radiates outward. Fill the center of the flower with a Twirled Ribbon Rose or French Knots. For Buttonhole Wheels, work the linked threads so that they form a neat finish around the outside edge.

Flowers
Work clockwise.

Bring needle up at **1**, down at **2**, and up at **3**, just right of **1** on inner circle, with thread beneath needle. Repeat around circle, spacing as required. Stitches may be arranged to radiate regularly or irregularly. Move insertion point off-center for a less formal effect, or make petals of different lengths.

Wheels
Work counterclockwise, turning the work as stitching proceeds.

Bring needle up on edge of circle, down at center, up again a short distance along the edge with thread beneath needle as shown. Pull through gently. Repeat all around. Form last stitch by passing needle under first stitch (at **1**) and inserting needle at center as before.

Move insertion point off-center for a less formal effect.

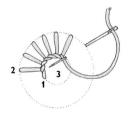

Knotted Blanket Stitch

This is also a Buttonhole Stitch, but with a knot worked at the end. It may be worked evenly in rows, curved to form circles, or fanned out to suggest more natural forms. It is used as a decorative edging, for borders, or for the stems of small flowers. Working from left to right, the twisted edge forms along the lower line, with the knots on the upper line.

Fig A Bring needle up at **1** at left end of lower line. Loop thread around left thumb and insert needle through loop from below.

Fig B Slip loop from thumb onto needle and insert needle at **2** on the upper line, bringing it out again at **3** directly below, with thread beneath needle tip as shown. Pull through, holding knot in place with left thumb.

Fig C Repeat to the right.

Stitches may be arranged in circles or curves, fanning evenly or irregularly.

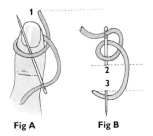

Fig A   **Fig B**

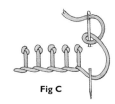

Fig C

Back Stitch

Horizontal Back Stitch
Work from right to left.

Fig A Bring needle up at **1**, down at **2**, one thread to right, up at **3**, one thread to left of **1**, and down at **1**. Repeat this stitch to the left.

Vertical Back Stitch
Work from top to bottom.

Fig B Bring needle up at **1**, down at **2**, one thread above, up at **3**, one thread below **1**, and down at **1**. Repeat this stitch down the canvas.

Split Stitch

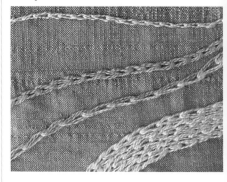

Work from left to right.

Bring needle up at **1** and down at **2**. Pull through firmly. Bring needle up again at **3**, through the center of the thread. Repeat as required.

Two-color Split Stitch
Thread needle with two colors. When splitting stitches, always keep one color above the needle and the other below.

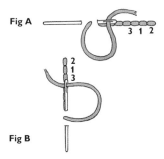

Fig A

Fig B

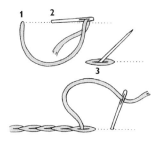

Note Illustrated as ● in Motif Library.

Note Illustrated as ● in Motif Library.

126

Bullion Knot

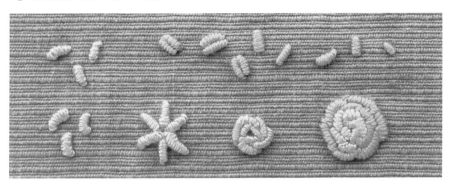

This stitch may be worked using narrow ribbon or embroidery thread, and is also known as Caterpillar, Worm, Coil, Roll, or Post Stitch. Use it alone to represent the stamen of a flower such as a lily, scatter it throughout a design to add texture, or work it in a flower or a star shape. Work in any direction.

Fig A Bring needle up at **1** and down at **2**. Pull through, leaving a long loop of thread.

Fig B Bring needle point up at **1**, and twist thread around point, five to eight times. Hold

twists in place with left hand and pull needle through.

Fig C Hold thread toward **2** and pack twists down with needle tip.

Fig D Take needle through at **2**.

Bullion Knot Rose
Fig E Begin roses with a triangle of Bullion Knots. Work next knot around one corner, adding extra twists to make it curl. Continue adding overlapping knots as desired.

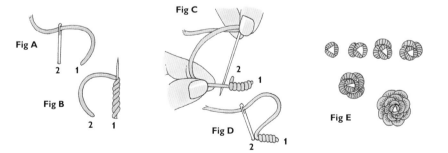

Note Illustrated as ▓▓▓ in Motif Library.

Shaded Satin Stitch

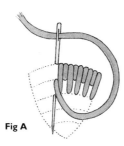

Fig A

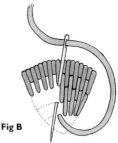

Fig B

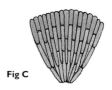

Fig C

Fig A Begin at center of outside edge with a line of long and short Satin Stitches. Work from center to right, then return to the center and work to the left. Always bring the needle up inside the shape and insert it at the edge. Point all stitches toward the center of the lower edge in a fan arrangement.

Fig B With another shade, work stitches to fit between those above. If the shape tapers sharply, miss out some stitches. Make the lower edge of this line alternately long and short with stitches of different lengths. (Repeat this row as required.)

Fig C At the lower edge, make long and short stitches as necessary to complete the shape.

Note Illustrated as 🪶 in Motif Library.

Pendant Couching

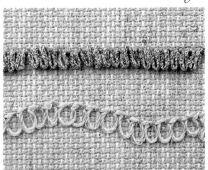

Scale Couching

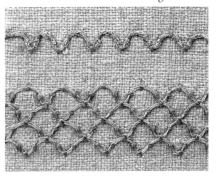

Open Loop Pendant Couching

Work from right to left.

Fig A Bring laid thread up at right. Make a small tying stitch from **1** to **2**. Arrange laid thread in a small loop and make another tying stitch close to the first. Repeat. At end of line, fasten both threads at the back of the fabric.

Closed Loop Pendant Couching

Fig B Work as above, but arrange laid thread in closed loops, with tying stitches over double thread at top of each loop.

Begin at top left.

Bring laid thread up at left. Bring tying thread up at **1** and down at **2**, over laid thread. Hold laid thread in a small curve and make two more tying stitches, **3** to **4** and **5** to **6**. Repeat to right.

At edge, laid thread may be taken to wrong side and brought back to begin next line, or turned in a curve on the surface. Work next line from right to left, alternating with scales above. Fasten both threads at back of fabric.

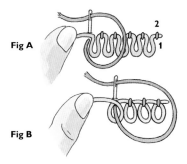

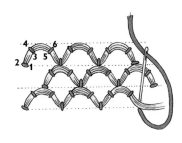

Woven and Whipped Circles

This woven stitch is used to produce small circular motifs with a raised appearance, and is also known as Spider Web Stitch or Ribbed Wheel Filling. Fine, narrow ribbon or embroidery thread may be used. Leave spikes around the edge of the outline, or fill it completely. For effective "stars" in a night sky, use silver embroidery thread.

Woven Circle
Fig A Work on an odd number (start with seven) of radiating stitches. Mark fabric with a circle and a center dot, then divide the circle with evenly spaced dots. Bring needle up at outside and insert it at center to work these stitches.

Bring a blunt needle up at **1**.

Fig B Weave over first thread and under next; repeat as required. Pull the first round quite tightly to close up the center, but make later rounds looser to lie flat. When weaving is complete, insert needle under previous round of weaving (for example, at **2**).

Whipped Circle
Fig C Work on any number of radiating stitches, made as for Woven Circles. Bring blunt needle up at **1**. Pass needle under first thread, back over this thread, and under both first and second threads.

Fig D Pass back over one thread and under two threads. Repeat as required. End as for Woven Circle.

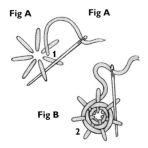

Fig A   Fig A

Fig B

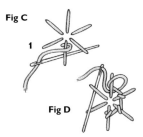

Fig C

Fig D

Shisha Stitch

This is also known as Indian Mirror Stitch. For contemporary designs, it may be used to appliqué objects including small mirrors, shells, or metal shapes to the fabric.

Fig A Hold disc in place with left thumb. Bring needle up at **1**, down at **2**, up at **3**, down at **4**, and up at **5**. Pass under first stitch from top to bottom, then under second stitch in same way as shown, and insert at **6**.

Fig B Bring needle up at **7** and pass under second stitch from bottom to top, then under first stitch in same way, inserting needle at **8**. These four stitches hold the disc in place. Bring needle up at **9**.

Fig C Pass needle under first intersection of holding stitches with working thread to left. Pull through.

Fig D Insert needle at **9** and bring it out at **10**, with thread under needle to form an Open Chain Stitch (*see page 83*). Pull through.

Fig E Pass needle under single holding stitch, with thread to left of needle, pull through.

Fig F Insert needle at **10**, make another Open Chain Stitch along edge, bringing needle out at **11**. Repeat around edge of disc, working inner stitches over both threads at intersections of holding stitches. Fasten off last Open Chain Stitch with a tiny stitch.

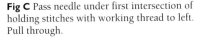

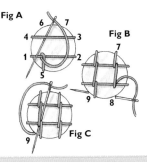

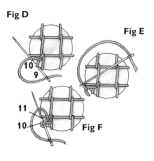

Applying Beads and Sequins

Beads and sequins are used in both traditional and contemporary ribbon embroidery. Sequins are produced in many different shapes and sizes, including stars, flowers, shells, hearts, and birds. They may be attached individually using a single seed bead, or in rows using invisible stitches. They make effective borders and frames.

Sewing on sequins with Back Stitch

The stitching is visible, and therefore best treated as a decorative feature, perhaps with a contrasting thread. Work from right to left.

Fig A Bring needle up at **1** through fabric and thread sequin onto needle. Make a Back Stitch, taking needle down at **2** just over the right edge of the sequin, and up at **3** to attach next sequin. Distance between **1** and **3** is width of one sequin, so that the sequins are just touching.

Sewing on sequins with invisible stitches

Here the sequins are overlapped to hide the stitches. Use thread of a color to blend with the sequins. Work from right to left.

Fig B Bring thread up through fabric at **1** and thread sequin onto needle. Make a Back Stitch over the left side of the sequin, taking needle

down at **2** and up at **3** to attach next sequin. Distance between **1** and **3** is half the width of one sequin, so the sequins overlap and the Back Stitches are hidden. Repeat to the left.

Sewing on sequins with continuous stitches

This method holds the sequins more firmly, and flat against the fabric. Work from right to left.

Fig C Bring needle up at **1** and thread first sequin onto needle. Make a Back Stitch, taking needle down at **2**, just over right edge of sequin, and up at **3** on left edge of sequin, and make a second Back Stitch, inserting needle back through center of sequin at **1** and bringing it out again at **4** to begin next repeat.

Fig A
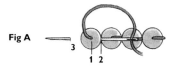

Fig B
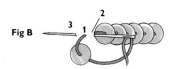

Fig C
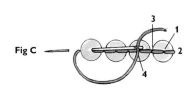

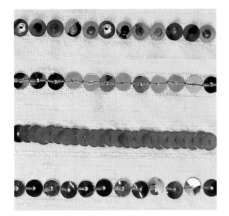

Sewing on sequins using beads

Tiny seed beads may be used to attach sequins individually or in rows. Choose beads of a matching or contrasting color, with thread to match. Work from right to left.

Fig D Bring needle up through fabric at required position and thread a sequin onto needle. Then thread the bead onto needle and insert needle back through center of sequin. Pull firmly so the bead holds the sequin in place. Bring needle out at position for center of next sequin. Repeat as required.

Couching beads

Two threads are used, the first on which the beads are strung, and the second to stitch down the first.

Fig E Bring up first thread through fabric at **1**. Thread on beads as required and "park" needle in a convenient position.

Thread another needle, hold first bead in place, and bring needle up at **2**, close to first bead. Insert needle at **3** tying down first thread and holding first bead in place. Repeat as required. At end of line take first thread through to wrong side of work and secure firmly.

Fig D

Fig E

Tête-de-boeuf Stitch

Work in any direction.

First work a Detached Chain Stitch (*see page 65*). Then add two Straight Stitches: Bring needle up at **1**, down at **2**, up at **3**, and down at **4**. Repeat as necessary.

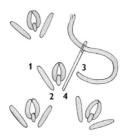

Blanket Stitch

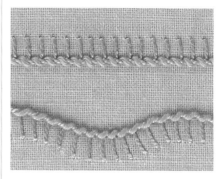

This versatile stitch may be worked open or closed, using narrow ribbon or decorative threads and yarns. In ribbon embroidery, it may be used as a decorative border, worked in straight, even lines, or curved for more informal designs. Working from left to right, the twisted edge forms at the lower line.

Fig A Bring needle up at **1**, down at **2**, and up at **3**, with thread looped under needle. Pull through. Take care to tighten the stitches equally throughout for a neat twisted edge.

Fig B Repeat to the right. Fasten down the last loop by taking a small stitch along the lower line.

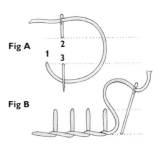

Appliqué

Appliqué is a technique for attaching fabric shapes to a background of another fabric, and is a fast, simple way to achieve bold, dramatic effects. It is a useful way to add larger images or areas of texture to a ribbon embroidery piece. Most fabrics are suitable, but avoid stretchy fabric, that may distort, or coarsely woven fabrics, that may fray. Printed motifs, or shapes cut from fabrics such as organza and lace, are ideal. Attach the shapes using matching thread and tiny stitches, perhaps a chain or blanket stitch. They may also be attached by machine, or fused to the background fabric using fine bonding web.

For work that is easy to handle, choose closely woven fabrics of similar weights. To prevent fraying and eliminate the need to cover raw edges completely, use fusible bonding. To prevent fraying on a fabric that a hot iron might damage, such as velvet, a synthetic, or PVC, outline the edge with fabric paint, use a stitch such as Buttonhole Stitch, or Couch with decorative thread. For a three-dimensional effect, press the cut edges of the shape under and use small invisible hemming stitches to catch the edge of the fold to the fabric.

Fusible bonding

This is a web of heat-sensitive fiber that stiffens the work slightly and makes it easier to handle. To use, remove the paper backing and place it on the wrong side of an appliqué shape, then fuse it to the background using a hot iron. For heat settings and ironing times, refer to the manufacturer's instructions.

Motif Library

The Motif Library is the most exciting section of the book, containing over 50 original designs by professional teachers and designers. Work the patterns as they are or integrate them into your own designs. The Library caters to a range of embroidery skills; simpler designs for the beginner appear first, followed by intermediate, and then more advanced motifs for the more adventurous embroiderer.

Balloons

The choice of color used in an embroidery design will often suggest a theme. The monochromatic blue-toned color scheme in this motif suggests the celebration at the birth of a baby boy. By stitching the image in alternative colors, it may be used for a variety of special occasions.

YOU WILL NEED

Fabric
Linen
10 x 12 in.
(25 x 31cm)

Needles
Assorted chenille needles,
sizes 18 to 24

Beading needle

Embroidery thread
Blue

White

Silk ribbon
Mint green 2mm

Dark blue 4mm

Light blue 4mm

Cream 4mm

Baby blue 7mm

Organza ribbon
Baby blue 15mm

Beads
Small glass beads

Sequins
Small bird-shaped sequins

PATTERN GUIDE

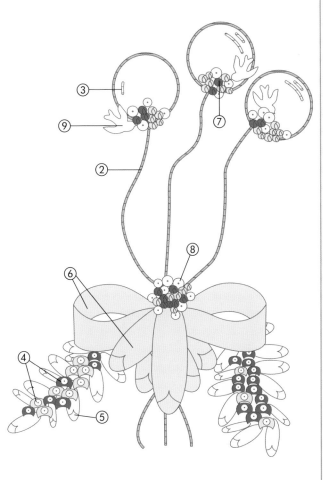

ORDER OF WORK

① Stretch the fabric on a hoop. Transfer pattern to fabric.

Balloons

② Outline balloons and strings using two strands of blue thread and Stem Stitch.

③ Work "reflection marks" on balloons in Stem Stitch using two strands of white thread.

Floral swags

④ Work using dark and light blue 4mm ribbon and Looped Straight Stitch. Sew a bead into the center of each loop.

Leaves

⑤ Work using mint green 2mm and cream 4mm ribbon and Ribbon Stitch.

Bow

⑥ Make a bow using the organza ribbon. Work the ties using baby blue 7mm ribbon and Ribbon Stitch.

Details

⑦ Work French Knots at the base of each balloon and at the top of the bow using dark blue and light blue 4mm ribbon.

⑧ Scatter beads among the French Knots.

⑨ Attach three bird sequins to the balloons.

KEY TO STITCHES USED

 Stem Stitch, *page 94*

Looped Straight Stitch, *page 59*

Ribbon Stitch, *page 63*

French Knot, *page 70*

Closed Iris

Simple, uncluttered motifs may be used alone to decorate linen or more personal items. The motif illustrated here may also be combined with additional ribbon embroidery motifs and stitches to make a more complex design.

YOU WILL NEED

Fabric

Linen
10 x 12 in.
(25 x 31cm)

Needles

Assorted chenille needles, sizes 18 to 24

Beading needle

Embroidery thread

Pale green

Taupe

Silk ribbon

Mint green 2mm

Green 7mm

Cream 7mm

Yellow 7mm

Gold 7mm

Organza ribbon

Aqua 5mm

Beads

Pearl beads

Clear glass beads

PATTERN GUIDE

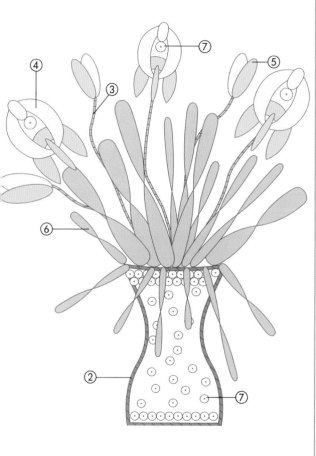

ORDER OF WORK

(1) Stretch the fabric on a hoop. Transfer pattern to fabric.

Vase

(2) Outline using two strands of taupe thread and Stem Stitch.

Stems

(3) Work using two strands of pale green thread and Stem Stitch.

Flower heads

(4) Work using cream, yellow, and gold 7mm ribbon and Closed Iris stitch. Add an additional Straight Stitch at the base of each stitch.

Buds

(5) Place two Straight Stitches, one in cream and the other in either yellow or gold 7mm ribbon, side by side.

Leaves

(6) Work using mint green 2mm ribbon, green 7mm ribbon, and aqua organza 5mm ribbon, and Twisted Straight Stitch.

Details

(7) Embellish vase and flower heads with pearl and clear glass beads.

KEY TO STITCHES USED

Stem Stitch, *page 94*

Closed Iris, *page 99*

Straight Stitch, *page 58*

Twisted Straight Stitch, *page 60*

Silk and Organza Daisies

This bright, pretty motif, using simple Padded
Straight Stitch, has been designed for the novice
embroiderer. Organza ribbons have been stitched
over silk ribbon to give a fragile and delicate
texture to the embroidered petals.

YOU WILL NEED

Fabric

Pure cotton
11¾ x 11¾ in.
(30 x 30cm)

Needles

Assorted crewel needles,
sizes 1 to 10

Assorted chenille needles,
sizes 13 to 26

Embroidery thread

Green

Silk ribbon

Green 2mm

Light red 4mm

Pale lavender 4mm

Lavender 4mm

Medium fuchsia 4mm

Dark peach 4mm

Organza ribbon

Rose 5mm

Orchid 5mm

Magenta 5mm

Chamois 5mm

ORDER OF WORK

① Stretch the fabric on a hoop. Transfer pattern to fabric.

Flowers

② Work the flowers in Padded Straight Stitch. Use silk ribbons for the base stitch and organza ribbons for the top stitch in combinations as follows:
Flower A: Lavender 4mm and orchid 5mm
Flower B: Medium fuchsia 4mm and rose 5mm
Flower C: Dark peach 4mm and chamois 5mm
Flower D: Pale lavender 4mm and orchid 5mm
Flower E: Lavender 4mm and rose 5mm
Flower F: Light red 4mm and magenta 5mm
Flower G: Pale lavender 4mm and rose 5mm

Buds

③ Work the buds in Padded Straight Stitch, again using silk ribbons for the base stitch and organza ribbon for the top stitch, in combinations as follows:
Bud H: Dark peach 4mm and chamois 5mm
Bud I: Lavender 4mm and rose 5mm
Bud J: Pale lavender 4mm and orchid 5mm
Bud K: Light red 4mm and magenta 5mm

PATTERN GUIDE

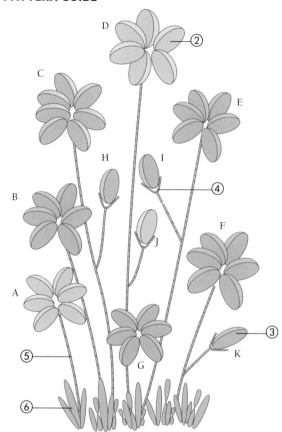

Foliage

④ Work the bud calyxes in Fly Stitch using green embroidery thread.

⑤ Work the stems in Stem Stitch using green embroidery thread.

⑥ Use green 2mm ribbon to work the grass at the base of the flowers in a mixture of Straight Stitch and Twisted Straight Stitch.

KEY TO STITCHES USED

 Padded Straight Stitch, *page 61*

Fly Stitch, *page 62*

Stem Stitch, *page 94*

Straight Stitch, *page 58*

Twisted Straight Stitch, *page 60*

Flowering Barrow

Spider Web Roses are possibly the easiest to
master of all the rose stitches. As woven
stitches, they are quick to make and fill
in a basic design with very pleasing
results. This flowering barrow is
a simple image that may be
embroidered as a border on
linen hand towels or perhaps
an apron.

YOU WILL NEED

Fabric

Linen
11¾ x 11¾ in.
(30 x 30cm)

Needles

Assorted crewel needles,
sizes 1 to 10

Assorted chenille needles,
sizes 13 to 26

Embroidery thread

Variegated pink/purple

Silk ribbon

Cream 4mm

Purple 4mm

Medium blue 4mm

Aqua 4mm

Mauve 7mm

Organza ribbon

Rose 5mm

Crimson 5mm

PATTERN GUIDE

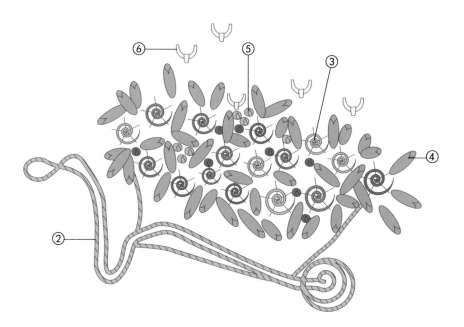

ORDER OF WORK

① Stretch the fabric on a hoop. Transfer pattern to fabric.

Outline

② Outline the wheelbarrow using Stem Stitch and two strands of variegated pink/purple thread.

Roses

③ Work Spider Web Roses where indicated, in a variety of colored ribbons: Purple 4mm, medium blue 4mm, rose 5mm organza, crimson 5mm organza, and mauve 7mm ribbon.

Leaves

④ Stitch the leaves using Ribbon Stitch and aqua 4mm ribbon.

⑤ Fill in any gaps between the leaves and the roses with French Knots in rose 5mm organza and crimson 5mm organza ribbon.

Insects

⑥ Stitch the insects using Fly Stitch and cream 4mm ribbon.

KEY TO STITCHES USED

 Stem Stitch, page 94
Spider Web Rose, page 112
 Ribbon Stitch, page 63

 French Knot, page 70
Fly Stitch, page 62

Naïve Lily Pond

The naïve style is used in many art forms. It is a design style that is used to capture a single moment in time and offers a simplistic, almost childlike, view of the world. The lily pond illustrated here is an excellent example.

YOU WILL NEED

Fabric

Polyester silk
11¾ x 11¾ in.
(30 x 30cm)

Needles

Chenille needle, size 24

Fine embroidery needle

Embroidery thread

Leaf green

Light blue

Silk ribbon

Dark green 2mm

Light brown 4mm

Light green 4mm

Dark brown 4mm

Organza ribbon

Pink 4mm

Blue 4mm

PATTERN GUIDE

ORDER OF WORK

① Stretch fabric on a hoop. Transfer pattern to fabric.

Cattails

② Work the heads of the cattails in Straight Stitch using dark brown 4mm ribbon.

③ Work the stems using two strands of leaf green thread and one long Straight Stitch.

④ Use Twisted Straight Stitch and dark green 2mm ribbon to create the leaves.

Lily pond

⑤ Work the lily pond edge in Back Stitch using two strands of light blue thread.

Butterflies

⑥ Make the wings of the butterflies using Detached Chain Stitch, working four wings for each butterfly. For two of the butterflies,

use blue 4mm organza ribbon; for the other, use pink 4mm organza.

⑦ Create each of the bodies using one Straight Stitch in light brown 4mm ribbon.

Grass

⑧ Work the grass in a mixture of Straight Stitches and Twisted Straight Stitches using light green 4mm ribbon.

Waterlilies

⑨ Work the stem linking the waterlilies in Straight Stitch and two strands of leaf green thread.

⑩ Stitch the leaves in Detached Chain Stitch and dark green 2mm ribbon.

⑪ Work the flowers in small Detached Chain Stitches and pink 4mm organza ribbon.

KEY TO STITCHES USED

 Straight Stitch, *page 58*

Twisted Straight Stitch, *page 60*

Back Stitch, *page 126*

Detached Chain Stitch, *page 65*

Holiday Wreath

This motif would make a pretty border encircling a
personal message or festive image. It would look
delightful worked on linen napkins, and could be
reduced in size and stitched to border name cards
for a truly personalized table setting.

YOU WILL NEED

Fabric

Polyester silk
10 x 12 in.
(25 x 31cm)

Needles

Assorted chenille needles,
sizes 18 to 24

Beading needle

Silk ribbon

Dark green 2mm

Medium green 7mm

Red 13mm

Beads

Red glass beads

PATTERN GUIDE

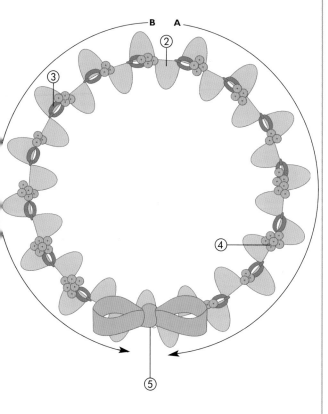

ORDER OF WORK

① Stretch the fabric on a hoop. Transfer pattern to fabric.

Leaves

② Work Gathered Ribbon Leaves in the directions shown (see arrows A and B), starting at the top of the wreath and using medium green 7mm ribbon.

③ Fill in the gathered leaf design with smaller leaves using dark green 2mm ribbon and Detached Chain Stitch.

Details

④ Attach red glass beads for the berries.

⑤ Attach a small bow using red 13mm ribbon.

KEY TO STITCHES USED

 Gathered Ribbon Leaf, *page 90*

 Detached Chain Stitch, *page 65*

Beaded Holiday Wreath

This wreath is stitched in Straight Stitch with red beads used to form the centers. Although a holiday motif has been stitched here, the pattern may be easily worked into other designs. It is ideal for borders.

YOU WILL NEED

Fabric

Linen
10 x 12 in.
(24 x 31cm)

Needles

Assorted tapestry needles, sizes 18 to 24

Beading needle

Embroidery thread

Invisible thread

Silk ribbon

Dark green 4mm

Red 4mm

Beads

Medium red glass

Small red glass

ORDER OF WORK

① Stretch the fabric on a hoop. Transfer pattern to fabric.

Leaves

② Using dark green 4mm ribbon and Straight Stitch, form six-petaled daisies around the circle, leaving an open center for each. Ensure the center of each is on the line of the circle.

Beads

③ Attach the beads to the center of each daisy as follows: bring invisible thread up from the back of the fabric. String a medium red bead onto the thread, followed by a small bead. Take the thread back through the large bead and back through the fabric. Pull the thread so that the larger bead is lying flat and the small bead is on its side. Either fasten the thread at the back of the fabric or continue to the next daisy center. Leave one flower center at the bottom right of the design without any beading.

Bow

④ Form the bow using the red 4mm ribbon. Take the needle into the fabric through the center of the flower without beading, leaving enough ribbon to tie the bow. Bring the needle back up through the fabric again close to the entry point. Remove

PATTERN GUIDE

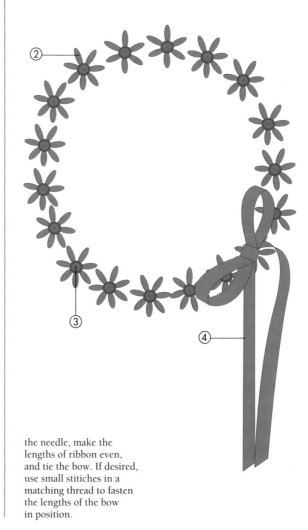

the needle, make the lengths of ribbon even, and tie the bow. If desired, use small stitiches in a matching thread to fasten the lengths of the bow in position.

KEY TO STITCHES USED

Straight Stitch, page 58

Sunflower

This sunflower was designed by the artist in
memory of her father, and represents
warmth, light, and the celebration of life. The
center of the flower is beaded but it may
also be stitched with French or
Colonial Knots.

YOU WILL NEED

Fabric

Polyester silk
11¾ x 11¾ in.
(30 x 30cm)

Needles

Assorted chenille needles,
sizes 13 to 26

Beading needle

Silk ribbon

Dark brown 4mm

Medium brown 4mm

Gold 4mm

Yellow 4mm

Beads

Bronze seed beads

PATTERN GUIDE

ORDER OF WORK

① Stretch the fabric on a hoop. Transfer pattern to fabric.

Center

② Using a matching thread, fill the central circle entirely with a spiral of bronze seed beads. Alternatively, stitch French Knots using bronze embroidery thread.

Petals

③ Work all the medium brown petals in Detached Chain Stitch using medium brown 4mm ribbon.

④ Work all the dark brown petals in Detached Chain Stitch using dark brown 4mm ribbon.

⑤ Work all the gold petals in Detached Chain Stitch using gold 4mm ribbon.

⑥ Work all the outer yellow petals in Straight Stitch using yellow 4mm ribbon.

KEY TO STITCHES USED

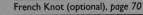 French Knot (optional), *page 70*

Detached Chain Stitch, *page 65*

 Straight Stitch, *page 58*

Poinsettias

This traditional flower blooms in winter in the United States, Canada, and Europe, and has become associated with the holiday season. These bright and cheerful flower motifs will certainly brighten the home on even the coldest of winter days.

YOU WILL NEED

Fabric

Linen
10 x 12 in.
(25 x 31cm)

Needles

Assorted tapestry needles, sizes 18 to 24

Embroidery thread

Gold metallic

Silk ribbon

Red 7mm

Green 4mm

PATTERN GUIDE

ORDER OF WORK

① Stretch the fabric on a hoop. Transfer pattern to fabric.

Petals

② Work the petals where marked in Straight Stitch using red 7mm ribbon.

Leaves

③ Use green 4mm ribbon and Straight Stitch to work the leaves.

Centers

④ Work the poinsettia centers with groups of French Knots in gold metallic thread.

KEY TO STITCHES USED

Straight Stitch, *page 58*

French Knot, *page 70*

155

Poppies

This is a popular flower design suitable for a novice stitcher to practice gathering and ribbon manipulation techniques. The stamens used here may be purchased from craft or florist suppliers. Alternatively, work the stamens using extended French Knots in black stranded cotton.

YOU WILL NEED

Fabric

Pure silk dupioni
11¾ x 11¾ in.
(30 x 30cm)

Needles

Crewel needles, sizes 1 to 3

Assorted tapestry needles, sizes 13 to 26

Assorted chenille needles, sizes 13 to 26

Beading needle

Embroidery thread

Green

Silk ribbon

Olive green 2mm

Olive green 7mm

Black 7mm

Red 7mm

Red 13mm

Beads

Medium black beads

Black flower stamens

ORDER OF WORK

(1) Stretch the fabric on a hoop. Transfer pattern to fabric.

Flowers

(2) Cut seven 4⅜ in. (11cm) lengths of both red 13mm ribbon and black 7mm ribbon. Lay them together with bottom edges together and work Gathered Ribbon Flowers. Attach each to the fabric where indicated.

(3) For each flower, take three black flower stamens, fold in half, and stitch down into each flower center. Stitch three medium black beads into each center to cover the base.

Bud

(4) Work the bud by gathering the bottom edge of a 1 in. (3cm) length of red 13mm ribbon and fasten it to the fabric where indicated.

(5) Work the calyx using a Fly Stitch and olive green 7mm ribbon.

Foliage

(6) Using green embroidery thread, work the stems in long Straight Stitches. Take the Straight Stitch from the base of each flower down to where the bow will be, then work another Straight Stitch radiating out from that point.

PATTERN GUIDE

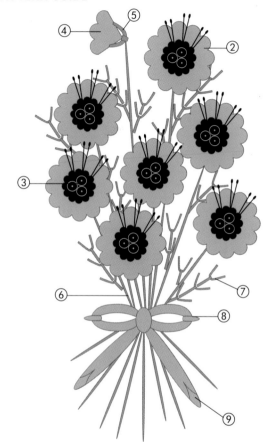

(7) Work the leaves in olive green 2mm ribbon and Fly Stitches in vertical rows.

Bow

(8) Using red 7mm ribbon, stitch two large Detached Chain Stitches for the loops of the bow.

(9) Work two long Ribbon Stitches for the bow tails and finish the bow with a small Straight Stitch in the center.

KEY TO STITCHES USED

 Gathered Ribbon Flower, *page 92*

Fly Stitch, *page 62*

Straight Stitch, *page 58*

 Detached Chain Stitch, *page 65*

Ribbon Stitch, *page 63*

157

Rainbow Daisies

A variegated rayon knitting ribbon was used to work these multicolored daisies. The petals were stitched in Twisted Straight Stitch and, as the rayon ribbon was twisted, a curl formed naturally at the tip of the petal where the ribbon was taken back into the fabric.

YOU WILL NEED

Fabric

	Natural linen 11¾ x 11¾ in. (30 x 30cm)

Needles

Assorted tapestry needles, sizes 13 to 26
Assorted chenille needles, sizes 13 to 26

Embroidery thread

Green
Cream

Rayon knitting ribbon

Variegated 5mm

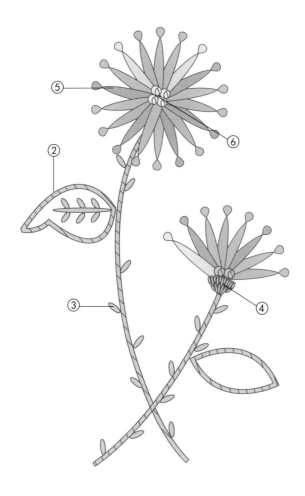

PATTERN GUIDE

ORDER OF WORK

①   Stretch the fabric on a hoop. Transfer pattern to fabric.

Stems and leaves

②   Stitch the stems and large leaves of the daisies in Stem Stitch using four strands of green embroidery thread.

③   Work the tiny leaves on the stalks and the vein details on the leaf of the large daisy in Straight Stitch.

④   Stitch the calyx on the small daisy in Satin Stitch. Add two French Knots above the calyx.

Daisies

⑤   Stitch the petals of the daisies in Twisted Straight Stitch using variegated 5mm rayon knitting ribbon. If necessary, manipulate the twist of the stitch so that it sits at the very end of the petal, forming a curl.

⑥   Stitch four French Knots using four strands of cream embroidery thread into the center of the large daisy.

KEY TO STITCHES USED

 Stem Stitch, *page 94*

 Straight Stitch, *page 58*

Satin Stitch, *page 84*

Twisted Straight Stitch, *page 60*

French Knot, *page 70*

Say It With Flowers

This simple design is ideal for the novice embroiderer. A combination of stitches is used, including Looped Straight Stitch, French Knots, Straight Stitch, Spider Web Roses, and Ribbon Stitch. It's the perfect design to embellish a gift card or to practice with before attempting more complicated motifs.

YOU WILL NEED

Fabric

Pure silk dupioni
11¾ x 11¾ in.
(30 x 30cm)

Needles

Assorted chenille needles,
sizes 13 to 26

Fine embroidery needle

Embroidery thread

Pink

Silk ribbon

Pink 4mm

Pale yellow 4mm

Dark green 4mm

Pale green 4mm

KEY TO STITCHES USED

 Straight Stitch, *page 58*

Looped Straight Stitch, *page 59*

French Knot, *page 70*

PATTERN GUIDE

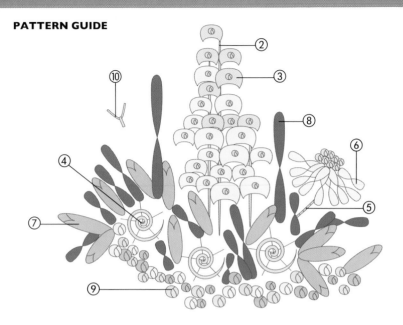

ORDER OF WORK

(1) Stretch the fabric on a hoop. Transfer pattern to fabric.

Snapdragons

(2) Stitch the stems of the snapdragon flowers in Straight Stitch using two strands of pink embroidery thread.

(3) Work the snapdragon flowers using pink 4mm and pale yellow 4mm ribbon in Looped Straight Stitch. Stitch French Knots into the centers of each loop with two strands of pink thread.

Roses

(4) Stitch the Spider Web Roses in pink 4mm ribbon.

Daisy

(5) Work the stem of the daisy in Stem Stitch using two strands of pink thread.

(6) Stitch the petals in Twisted Straight Stitch using pale yellow 4mm ribbon. Work four or five French Knots using pink 4mm ribbon for the center.

Foliage

(7) Stitch the short leaves in Ribbon Stitch using pale green 4mm ribbon.

(8) Work the longer grass stems in Twisted Straight Stitch using dark green 4mm ribbon.

(9) Around the base of the design, stitch French Knots using pale green 4mm, pink 4mm, and pale yellow 4mm ribbon.

(10) Stitch the little insect in Fly Stitch using two strands of pink thread.

 Spider Web Rose, *page 112*

Stem Stitch, *page 94*

Twisted Straight Stitch, *page 60*

 Ribbon Stitch, *page 63*

Fly Stitch, *page 62*

Climbing Flowers

This pretty motif may be stitched alone or incorporated into a more complex design. It would look stunning as a border on a small tablecloth. The Scrunched Gathered Flower technique (*see page 93*) has been used to form the flowers.

YOU WILL NEED

Fabric

Homespun/unbleached calico
11¾ x 11¾ in.
(30 x 30cm)

Needles

Assorted chenille needles,
sizes 13 to 26

Assorted crewel needles,
sizes 1 to 10

Embroidery thread

Green

Silk ribbon

Yellow 2mm

Blue 2mm

Lime green 4mm

Light khaki 4mm

Dark peach 4mm

Medium peach 4mm

Light peach 4mm

Pale apricot 4mm

Pink 7mm

Pale apricot 7mm

Light peach 7mm

Sundries

Short length of bronze metallic
lace ribbon OR bronze metallic
thread for Couching

ORDER OF WORK

(1) Stretch the fabric on a hoop. Transfer pattern to fabric.

Stems

(2) Work the stems using long Twisted Straight Stitches and light khaki 4mm ribbon.

Flowers

(3) Work the climbing flowers in ribbon combinations as follows:
Climber A: Pink 7mm and dark peach 4mm
Climber B: Pale apricot 7mm and light peach 4mm
Climber C: Light peach 7mm and medium peach 4mm
Climber D: Pink 7mm and pale apricot 4mm
Cut each ribbon into 2 in. (5cm) lengths. Match the ribbons up in the combinations shown above and lay each 4mm ribbon along the center of the 7mm ribbon. Use the Scrunched Gathered Flower method to form each of the separate flowers up the climbers.

Buds

(4) Stitch French Knot buds at the tips of the two central climbers using two ribbons threaded together through the needle, in the same size and color combination as the rest of the flowers on that climber.

PATTERN GUIDE

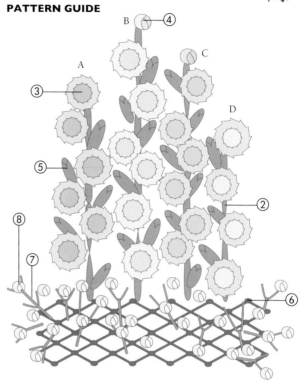

Leaves

(5) Work Ribbon Stitch leaves using lime green 4mm ribbon for the climber on the far left and light khaki 4mm on the other three climbers.

Base

(6) Tack a short length of bronze metallic lace ribbon to the base of the design OR Couch bronze metallic thread to the fabric using Scale or Pendant Couching.

(7) Use green thread to work random Fly Stitches over the base to suggest foliage.

(8) Work French Knot flowers among the green Fly Stitches using yellow 2mm and blue 2mm ribbon threaded together through the needle.

KEY TO STITCHES USED

 Twisted Straight Stitch, *page 60*

Scrunched Gathered Flower, *page 93*

French Knot, *page 70*

 Ribbon Stitch, *page 63*

 Scale/Pendant Couching (optional), *page 129*

Fly Stitch, *page 62*

Twirled Rose Keepsake

The subtle colors of the silk ribbons used
in this project lend themselves to the
romantic elements of this Victorian
design. This motif would make a beautiful
bridal keepsake worked on a silk bridal
ring pillow.

YOU WILL NEED

Fabric

Pure cotton
10 x 12 in.
(25 x 31cm)

Needles

Assorted chenille needles,
sizes 18 to 24

Beading needle

Silk ribbon

Pale green 4mm

Light pink 4mm

Medium pink 4mm

Salmon pink 7mm

Beads

Small glass beads

PATTERN GUIDE

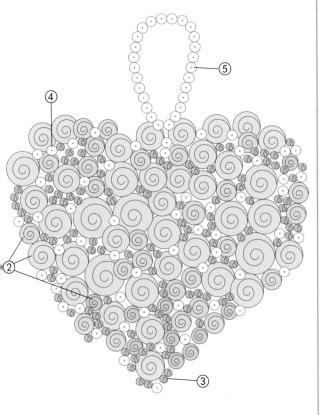

ORDER OF WORK

1. Stretch the fabric on a hoop. Transfer pattern to fabric.

Flower heads

2. Work roses using Twirled Ribbon Stitch and the light and medium pink 4mm ribbons and the salmon pink 7mm ribbon. Begin at the center and work toward the edges in circles.

Details

3. Fill gaps between roses with French Knots in pale green 4mm ribbon.
4. Attach beads between roses.
5. Work a bead loop at the top of the design.

KEY TO STITCHES USED

 Twirled Ribbon Rose, *page 114*

 French Knot, *page 70*

Rose Bouquet

The color of a rose given to a person in
the Victorian era always held certain
significance. Red roses symbolize eternal
love, respect, courage, and passion. This
design may be stitched in a variety of
different colored ribbons as a perfect way
to say "I love you," "Congratulations,"
"Thank you," or "Well done."

YOU WILL NEED

Fabric

Linen
10 x 12 in.
(25 x 31cm)

Needles

Assorted tapestry needles,
sizes 18 to 24

Embroidery thread

Green

Dark brown

Silk ribbon

Green 4mm

White 7mm

Red 7mm

PATTERN GUIDE

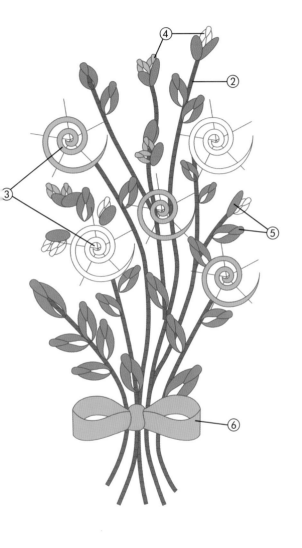

ORDER OF WORK

① Stretch the fabric on a hoop. Transfer pattern to fabric.

Stems
② Work in Stem Stitch using one strand each of dark brown and green thread.

Roses
③ Work three Spider Web Roses using red 7mm ribbon, and two using white 7mm ribbon.

Rosebuds
④ Add rosebuds using short Straight Stitch or short Detached Chain Stitch in either red or white 7mm ribbon.

Leaves
⑤ Work using green 4mm ribbon and Detached Chain Stitch. At the same time, add short Straight Stitches in the same ribbon around the buds to represent calyxes.

Bow
⑥ Take red 7mm ribbon down on the right side of the stems, leaving a 4 in. (10cm) tail. Bring it back up on the left side of the stems. Cut off, leaving a 4 in. (10cm) tail. Tie bow.

KEY TO STITCHES USED

 Stem Stitch, page 94

 Spider Web Rose, page 112

Straight Stitch, page 58

 Detached Chain Stitch, page 65

167

Seashell

This simple design uses several different fabrics. The base fabric is cream silk overlaid with green netting, the "seaweed" is stitched in organza ribbon, and the appliquéd shell is pale yellow silk.

YOU WILL NEED

Fabric

	Pure silk 12 x 10 in. (31 x 26cm) Netting 12 x 10 in. (31 x 26cm) Scraps of fabric for appliqué

Needles

Assorted chenille needles, sizes 18 to 24

Beading needle

Fabric paint outliner

Gold

White

Embroidery thread

Pale green

Silk ribbon

Salmon pink 4mm

Brown 4mm

Pale green 4mm

Peach 4mm

Ocher 4mm

Organza ribbon

Yellow 5mm

Green 5mm

Orange 5mm

Beads

Small pearl beads

PATTERN GUIDE

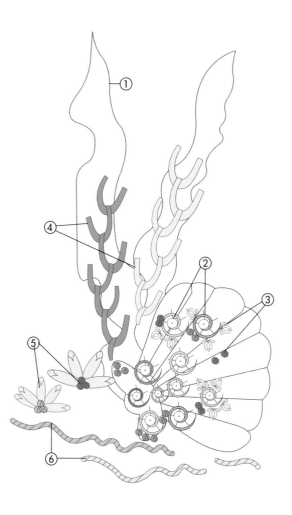

ORDER OF WORK

① Stretch fabric on hoop. Transfer seaweed and seashell shapes to fabric and outline with fabric paint and appliqué.

Flower and leaves

② Work Spider Web Roses on shell using salmon, peach, ocher, brown, and pale green 4mm ribbon, and yellow and orange 5mm organza ribbon. Sew a bead in the center of each.

③ Work in Detached Chain Stitch and two strands of pale green thread. Scatter French Knots around roses using brown, green, and peach 4mm ribbon.

Seaweed

④ Work in Chained Feather Stitch and green and yellow organza 5mm ribbon.

Seagrass

⑤ Work in Ribbon Stitch and yellow organza 5mm ribbon. Place three French Knots at the base of each tuft in either brown 4mm ribbon or two strands of pale green thread.

Sand

⑥ Work in Stem Stitch using pale green 4mm and yellow organza 5mm ribbon for the top ripple, and ocher 4mm ribbon for the lower one.

KEY TO STITCHES USED

Spider Web Rose, *page 112*		Chained Feather Stitch, *page 76*
Detached Chain Stitch, *page 65*		Ribbon Stitch, *page 63*
French Knot, *page 70*		Stem Stitch, *page 94*

Cornflowers

Beads and decorative threads are often used in
ribbon embroidery to add sparkle and a hint of
luxury to a design. The centers of these
cornflowers have been made using glass seed
beads. Alternatively, the centers may also be
stitched in French or Colonial Knots.

YOU WILL NEED

Fabric

Linen
10 x 12 in.
(25 x 31cm)

Needles

Assorted tapestry
needles, sizes 18 to 24

Beading needle

Embroidery thread

Invisible (for beading)

Silk ribbon

Green 4mm

Dark blue 4mm

Light blue 4mm

Beads

Gold glass beads

PATTERN GUIDE

ORDER OF WORK

(1) Stretch the fabric on a hoop. Transfer pattern to fabric.

Stems

(2) Work in green 4mm ribbon using Twisted Straight Stitch.

Leaves

(3) Work in green 4mm ribbon using long Ribbon Stitch.

Flowers

(4) For outer petals, work seven to nine Looped Straight Stitches in either dark or light blue 4mm ribbon (as shown in design). For inner petals, work five to seven Looped Straight Stitches in either dark or light blue 4mm ribbon (to contrast with the outer petals of each flower).

Centers

(5) Bring invisible thread through from the back of work, string six beads and take thread to the back. Bring to the front again and string five beads. Take thread to back and secure.

KEY TO STITCHES USED

 Twisted Straight Stitch, *page 60*

 Ribbon Stitch, *page 63*

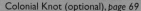 Looped Straight Stitch, *page 59*

 Colonial Knot (optional), *page 69*

Field Daisies

These daisies look wonderful in the background of a bouquet of flowers, or top-and-tailed to form a border. The flower petals were softened and made to look more realistic by overlapping long and short petals.

YOU WILL NEED

Fabric

Pure silk dupioni
10 x 12 in.
(25 x 31cm)

Needles

Chenille needles,
sizes 22 and 10

Embroidery thread

Yellow

Green

Silk ribbon

Olive green 2mm

White 2mm

Olive green 4mm

White 4mm

PATTERN GUIDE

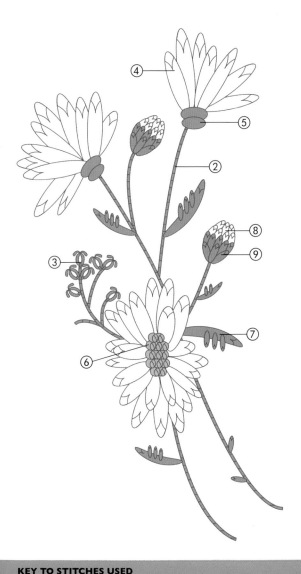

ORDER OF WORK

① Stretch the fabric on a hoop. Transfer pattern to fabric.

Stems and leaves

② Work the stems using Stem Stitch and one strand of green thread.

③ Add leaves to the branch using one strand of green thread and Detached Chain Stitch.

Daisies

④ Work petals using white 4mm ribbon and Ribbon Stitch.

⑤ Using olive green 4mm ribbon, work a Padded Straight Stitch at the base of each of the two half-daisies.

⑥ Using four strands of yellow thread, fill the center of the large daisy with French Knots.

Leaves

⑦ Work in Ribbon Stitch and olive green 2mm ribbon. Work small stitches into the edge.

Buds

⑧ Starting at the top with three stitches, work buds using white 2mm ribbon and Ribbon Stitch. Increase next row, stitching into previous row.

⑨ Change to olive green 2mm ribbon and work two rows, rounding into the base of flower.

KEY TO STITCHES USED

Stem Stitch, *page 94*

 Detached Chain Stitch, *page 65*

 Ribbon Stitch, *page 63*

Padded Straight Stitch, *page 61*

French Knot, *page 70*

Dragonfly

This is an excellent example of experimental stitching. The dragonfly is made using traditional stitches that have been modified by the artist to create this stunning, modern image. For a competent embroiderer who wishes to explore freestyle ribbon embroidery techniques, this would be an ideal starting point.

YOU WILL NEED

Fabric

Linen
10 x 12 in.
(25 x 31cm)

Needles

Assorted tapestry needles, sizes 18 to 24

Embroidery thread

Black
Purple metallic
Silver metallic

Silk ribbon

Gray 4mm
Pale purple 4mm
Lavender 4mm
Black 4mm

ORDER OF WORK

① Stretch the fabric on a hoop. Transfer pattern to fabric.

Wings

② Bring gray 4mm ribbon up at the edge of the dragonfly's body. Leaving a large loop that will outline the wings, take the ribbon down again next to the entry point. Do this for all four wings.

③ Baste the wings in place with two strands of silver metallic thread. Baste only until the ribbon will lie in place.

④ Within each wing, add two long Straight Stitches, one in pale purple 4mm and one in lavender 4mm ribbon.

⑤ To form the veins, add three or four long Straight Stitches in purple metallic thread over the top of the pale purple and lavender ribbon.

Head, body, and tail

⑥ Work the head using 4mm black ribbon and a French Knot.

⑦ Form the body using 4mm black ribbon and one long Straight Stitch. Continue on to form the tail using Running Stitch. Pull the last three stitches a bit tighter to make the end of the tail appear thinner.

⑧ Add eyes with French Knots using black embroidery thread.

PATTERN GUIDE

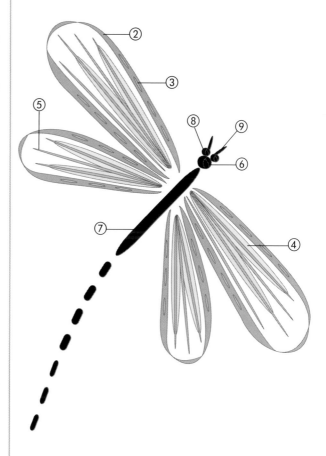

⑨ Add antennae using one strand of black embroidery thread and Straight Stitches.

KEY TO STITCHES USED

Straight Stitch, *page 58*

French Knot, *page 70*

Running Stitch, *page 73*

Celebration

As the floating hearts in the motif suggest, "Love is in the Air."
Ribbon Stitch, French Knots, and freestyle embroidery stitches
have been combined to create this quick and easy-to-make
design. It is suitable for Valentine's Day, anniversaries, and other
romantic occasions.

YOU WILL NEED

Fabric

Pure silk
10 x 12 in.
(25 x 31cm)

Needles

Assorted chenille needles,
sizes 18 to 24

Embroidery thread

Green

Red

Gold

Burgundy

Olive green

Silk ribbon

Olive green 2mm

Red 4mm

Crimson 4mm

Pink 4mm

Pale pink 4mm

Dark green 7mm

Olive green 7mm

Mid green 7mm

Light green 7mm

PATTERN GUIDE

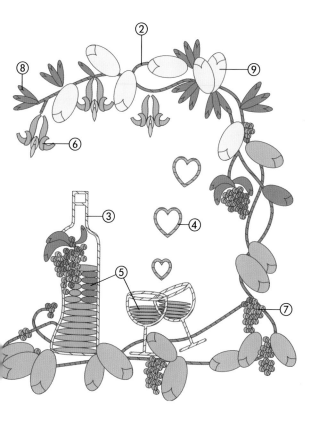

ORDER OF WORK

① Stretch the fabric on a hoop. Transfer pattern to fabric.

Outlines

② Outline vine using two strands of green thread and Stem Stitch.

③ Outline wine bottle using two strands of gold thread and Stem Stitch.

④ Outline hearts using two strands of red thread and Stem Stitch.

Wine

⑤ Fill in the wine in the bottle and the glasses using burgundy thread and Satin Stitch. Use olive green thread for the wine bottle label.

Bleeding Hearts

⑥ Work Bleeding Hearts using crimson and pale pink 4mm ribbon.

Grapes

⑦ Work in French Knots using red, crimson, and pink 4mm and olive green 2mm ribbon.

Leaves

⑧ Work Bleeding Heart leaves using olive green 2mm ribbon and Ribbon Stitch.

⑨ Work vine leaves using various shades of green 7mm ribbon and Ribbon Stitch.

KEY TO STITCHES USED

▬▬▬ Stem Stitch, *page 94*	Bleeding Heart, *page 107*
⬬ Satin Stitch, *page 84*	● French Knot, *page 70*
⬮ Ribbon Stitch, *page 63*	

Borders

Use borders to frame an
embroidered motif, or other
image. They may also be used
as a basic element to complement
a more complex design.
The borders shown here are
worked using traditional
embroidery stitches.

YOU WILL NEED

Fabric

Linen
10 x 12 in.
(25 x 31cm)

Needles

Assorted tapestry needles,
sizes 18 to 24

Beading needle

Embroidery thread

Invisible thread

Silk ribbon

Blue 4mm

Pink 4mm

Burgundy 4mm

White 7mm

Beads

Small pearl glass beads

PATTERN GUIDE

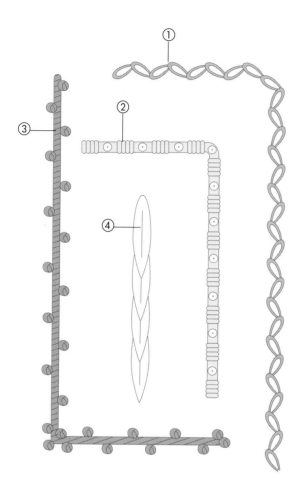

ORDER OF WORK

Four borders are shown here. Any color or width of ribbon may be used. They are worked as follows:

① This border, in blue 4mm ribbon, is worked in Chain Stitch in a zigzag pattern.

② This border is formed by Couching a length of gathered ribbon (pink 4mm) to the fabric with an invisible thread. Small pearl glass beads are stitched to the ribbon at each Couching stitch.

③ The burgundy 4mm border is worked in Stem Stitch. French Knots are staggered along either side of the border.

④ This border is worked using white 7mm ribbon and Split Stitch.

KEY TO STITCHES USED

Chain Stitch, page 122	French Knot, page 70
Couching, page 85	Split Stitch, page 126
Stem Stitch page 94	

Borders *continued*

When stitching a border, it is important to use stitches that can be linked to form a pleasing pattern. Consider the height and width of the stitches to be used in the border so that they remain balanced with the overall design.

YOU WILL NEED

Fabric

Linen
10 x 12 in.
(25 x 31cm)

Needles

Assorted tapestry needles, sizes 18 to 24

Silk ribbon

Light purple 4mm

Yellow 4mm

Green 4mm

Coral 4mm

PATTERN GUIDE

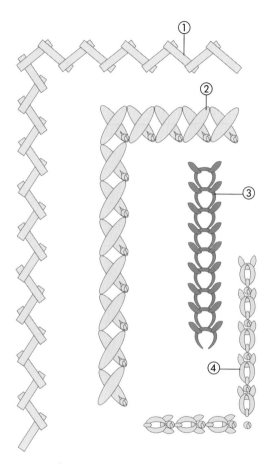

ORDER OF WORK

Four borders are shown here. Any color or width of ribbon may be used. They are worked as follows:

① This border is worked in light purple 4mm ribbon using Herringbone Stitch.

② This yellow 4mm ribbon border is worked in two stages. Firstly, a series of Ribbon Stitches are worked on the diagonal, with a French Knot added before piercing the ribbon. Then, these are worked over with a series of Straight Stitches worked on the opposite diagonal to form crosses.

③ This border is formed using green 4mm ribbon and Wheatear Stitch worked vertically.

④ This border, worked in coral 4mm ribbon, is formed with Closed Irises worked vertically. French Knots are placed between the Closed Irises and also when turning corners.

KEY TO STITCHES USED

 Herringbone Stitch, *page 82*

Ribbon Stitch, *page 63*

French Knot, *page 70*

Straight Stitch, *page 58*

 Closed Iris, *page 99*

Magical Garden

As a motif, this design could be used as a focal
point on which a more complex design may be
developed. Used alone, it would make a very
pretty special occasion card. Additional stitches
from the Stitch Collection may be added to
create a more personalized design.

YOU WILL NEED

Fabric

Pure silk
10 x 12 in.
(25 x 31cm)

Needles

Assorted chenille needles,
sizes 18 to 24

Embroidery thread

Tan

Olive green

Yellow

Silk ribbon

Yellow 2mm

Olive green 2mm

Dark green 2mm

Blue 2mm

Cream 4mm

Peach 4mm

Yellow 4mm

Orange 4mm

Red-brown 4mm

Leaf green 4mm

Light blue 4mm

Olive green 7mm

KEY TO STITCHES USED

Stem Stitch, *page 94*

Ribbon Stitch, *page 63*

ORDER OF WORK

① Stretch the fabric on a hoop. Transfer pattern to fabric.

Arch

② Using two strands of thread, use Stem Stitch to outline the arch and wall in tan and the grass in olive green.

③ Work the leaves using leaf green 4mm ribbon and Ribbon Stitch.

Snapdragons

④ Work the stalks in Straight Stitch and two strands of yellow thread.

⑤ Work the heads using orange and yellow 4mm ribbon and Looped Straight Stitch. Work the centers in French Knots using two strands of olive green thread.

Daisies

⑥ Work the daisy heads using red-brown 4mm ribbon and Detached Chain Stitch. Work the French Knot centers in peach 4mm ribbon.

Blue tulips

⑦ Work the stems using olive green 2mm ribbon and Twisted Straight Stitch. Work the leaves using olive green 2mm ribbon and twisted Ribbon Stitch. Work the heads using blue 2mm and light blue 4mm ribbon and Ribbon Stitch.

PATTERN GUIDE

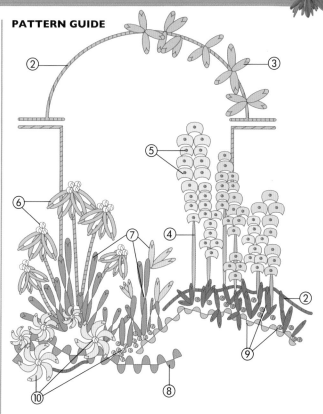

Foliage

⑧ Work foliage under the daisies by gathering a length of olive green 7mm ribbon along its center and stitching it to the fabric.

⑨ Work foliage under the snapdragons using dark green 2mm ribbon and Ribbon Stitch. Create grass by gathering a length of olive green 2mm ribbon and

attaching it to the fabric with small stitches. Scatter French Knots in red-brown 4mm ribbon.

Yellow flowers

⑩ Work using yellow 2mm and 4mm ribbon and Ribbon Stitch. Work French Knot centers in two strands of cream 4mm ribbon. Scatter French Knots in peach 4mm ribbon.

Straight Stitch, *page 58*	Detached Chain Stitch, *page 65*
Looped Straight Stitch, *page 59*	Twisted Straight Stitch, *page 60*
French Knot, *page 70*	

Alphabet
with Colonial Knot Roses

Monograms have always been popular, especially
when decorating gifts, and there are many
scripts available that lend themselves to being
embroidered. On the following pages, the
alphabet has been divided into groups of letters
with different floral designs. The floral designs
offered with each letter may be interchanged to
suit your personal taste or stitched together as
on page 196.

YOU WILL NEED

Fabric

Linen
10 x 12 in.
(25 x 31cm)

Needles

Assorted tapestry needles,
sizes 18 to 24

Embroidery thread

Green

Silk ribbon

Medium rose 4mm

Dark rose 4mm

Dark blue 4mm

Yellow 4mm

Green 4mm

PATTERN GUIDE

ORDER OF WORK

① Stretch the fabric on a hoop. Transfer pattern to fabric.

Letter
② Outline using three strands of green thread and Stem Stitch.

Flowers
③ Using two different colors of 4mm ribbon for each letter, work Colonial Knot roses.

Leaves
④ Work where indicated using green 4mm ribbon and Ribbon Stitch.

KEY TO STITCHES USED

Stem Stitch, *page 94*

Colonial Knot, *page 69*

Ribbon Stitch, *page 63*

Alphabet continued

with *Cornflowers and Apple Blossoms*

The cornflowers and apple blossoms illustrated on this page are very simple to master. The petals are formed by grouping small Looped Straight Stitches together. The flower is then completed with a neat French Knot in the center.

YOU WILL NEED

Fabric

Linen
10 x 12 in.
(25 x 31cm)

Needles

Assorted tapestry needles, sizes 18 to 24

Embroidery thread

Green

Silk ribbon

Light blue 4mm

Medium pink 4mm

Medium yellow 4mm

Green 4mm

PATTERN GUIDE

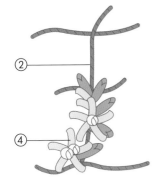

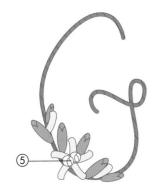

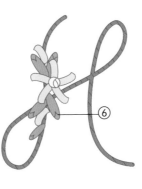

ORDER OF WORK

① Stretch the fabric on a hoop. Transfer pattern to fabric.

Letter
② Outline using three strands of green thread and Stem Stitch.

Apple blossom
③ Work the petals using medium pink 4mm ribbon and Looped Straight Stitch.

Cornflowers
④ Work the petals using light blue 4mm ribbon and Looped Straight Stitch.

Details
⑤ Fill the centers with French Knots using medium yellow 4mm ribbon.

Leaves
⑥ Work using green 4mm ribbon and Ribbon Stitch.

KEY TO STITCHES USED

Stem Stitch, *page 94*

Looped Straight Stitch, *page 59*

French Knot, *page 70*

Ribbon Stitch, *page 63*

Alphabet continued
with *Daisies and Black-eyed Susans*

By changing the color of ribbon used, a
variety of different flowers may be made
using the same stitches. Here, the flowers are
stitched using Twisted Straight Stitch. The
traditional daisy is stitched with white petals
and a yellow center. Change the color of the
petals to yellow and the center to dark brown
for a "Black-eyed Susan."

YOU WILL NEED

Fabric

Linen
10 x 12 in.
(25 x 31cm)

Needles

Assorted tapestry needles,
sizes 18 to 24

Embroidery thread

Green

Dark brown

Yellow

Silk ribbon

Medium yellow 4mm

White 4mm

Green 4mm

PATTERN GUIDE

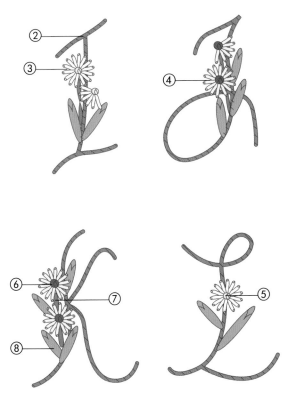

ORDER OF WORK

1. Stretch the fabric on a hoop. Transfer pattern to fabric.

Letter
2. Outline using three strands of green thread and Stem Stitch.

Daisies
3. Work the petals using white 4mm ribbon and Twisted Straight Stitch.

Black-eyed Susans
4. Work the petals using medium yellow 4mm ribbon and Twisted Straight Stitch.

Flower centers
5. Fill the centers of the Daisies with French Knots using yellow thread.
6. Fill the centers of the Black-eyed Susans with French Knots using dark brown thread.

Stems
7. Work using green 4mm ribbon and Twisted Straight Stitch.

Leaves
8. Stitch leaves using green 4mm ribbon and a lengthened Ribbon Stitch.

KEY TO STITCHES USED

Stem Stitch, *page 94*

Twisted Straight Stitch, *page 60*

 French Knot, *page 70*

Ribbon Stitch, *page 63*

Alphabet continued
with Pansies

Ribbon Stitch is one of the most frequently used
stitches in ribbon embroidery. It may be looped
(raised), twisted, padded, lengthened, shortened,
and curled to the left or right. The pansy petals
illustrated here may be worked in Ribbon Stitch
or Looped Straight Stitch.

YOU WILL NEED

Fabric

Linen
10 x 12 in.
(25 x 31cm)

Needles

Assorted tapestry needles,
sizes 18 to 24

Embroidery thread

Green

Dark brown

Yellow

White

Silk ribbon

Purple 4mm

Mauve 4mm

Medium yellow 4mm

Lemon yellow 4mm

Green 4mm

PATTERN GUIDE

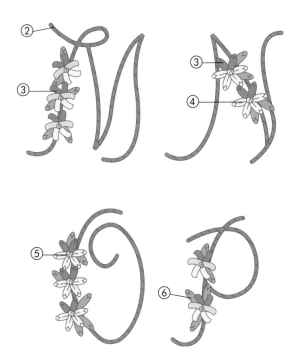

ORDER OF WORK

(1) Stretch the fabric on a hoop. Transfer pattern to fabric.

Letter

(2) Outline using three strands of green thread and Stem Stitch.

Pansy petals

(3) Work using either Looped Straight Stitch (see examples M and P) or Ribbon Stitch (see examples N and O). Begin with the top two petals in purple 4mm ribbon. Work the next two petals in mauve or medium yellow 4mm ribbon. Work the bottom two petals in either medium or lemon yellow 4mm ribbon.

Veins

(4) Using a single strand of dark brown thread, place veins on top of Ribbon Stitch petals or between Looped Straight Stitch petals.

Centers

(5) Fill centers with French Knots using one strand each of white and yellow thread.

Leaves

(6) Place leaves randomly using green 4mm ribbon and Ribbon Stitch.

KEY TO STITCHES USED

Stem Stitch, *page 94*

Looped Straight Stitch, *page 59*

 Ribbon Stitch, *page 63*

 French Knot, *page 70*

Alphabet continued
with Roses

The Spider Web Rose is the perfect rose for a
beginner to learn. It is a woven stitch that
requires very basic stitching skills. Despite
being a simple stitch it produces a very
beautiful flower. The size and width of the
petals is determined by the outline stitches
and the width of the ribbon used.

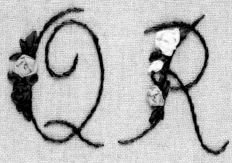

YOU WILL NEED

Fabric	
	Linen
	10 x 12 in.
	(25 x 31cm)

Needles	
	Assorted tapestry needles, sizes 18 to 24

Embroidery thread	
	Green

Silk ribbon	
	Light pink 4mm
	Dark pink 4mm
	Green 4mm
	White 7mm

PATTERN GUIDE

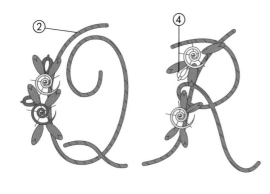

ORDER OF WORK

① Stretch the fabric on a hoop. Transfer pattern to fabric.

Letter

② Outline using three strands of green thread and Stem Stitch.

Roses

③ Work Spider Web Roses as indicated by the symbol using light pink or dark pink 4mm ribbon, or white 7mm ribbon.

Rosebuds

④ Work rosebuds in Detached Chain Stitch and either dark pink 4mm ribbon or white 7mm ribbon.

Leaves

⑤ Work in Ribbon Stitch using green 4mm ribbon.

KEY TO STITCHES USED

| Stem Stitch, *page 94* | Detached Chain Stitch, *page 65* |
| Spider Web Rose, *page 112* | Ribbon Stitch, *page 63* |

Alphabet continued
with *Canterbury Bells and Delphiniums*

French Knots and Ribbon Stitch are the
stitches used here to create these fragile
Canterbury bells and delphiniums. It is
important to use an even gauge and the
correct width ribbon to reproduce a
similar delicate effect.

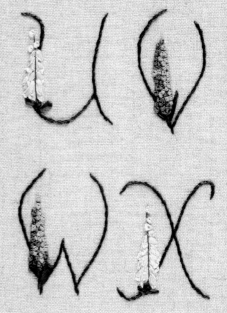

YOU WILL NEED

Fabric
Linen
10 x 12 in.
(25 x 31cm)

Needles
Assorted tapestry needles,
sizes 18 to 24

Embroidery thread
Green

Silk ribbon
Medium yellow 4mm

Light blue 4mm

Dark blue 4mm

Green 4mm

PATTERN GUIDE

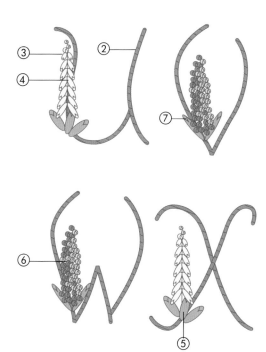

ORDER OF WORK

① Stretch the fabric on a hoop. Transfer pattern to fabric.

Letter

② Outline using three strands of green thread and Stem Stitch.

Canterbury Bells

③ Beginning at the bottom and working toward the top, work in Ribbon Stitch using medium yellow 4mm ribbon. Work three French Knots at the top of the flower with the same ribbon.

Stem

④ Using one strand of green thread, work as one long stitch coming up at the bottom and going back down under the top French Knot.

Canterbury Bell leaves

⑤ Work in green 4mm ribbon using long Ribbon Stitch.

Delphiniums

⑥ Work dark blue 4mm ribbon French Knots to halfway up one side. Change to light blue 4mm ribbon to complete.

Delphinium leaves

⑦ Work using green 4mm ribbon and Ribbon Stitch.

KEY TO STITCHES USED

Stem Stitch, *page 94*

Ribbon Stitch, *page 63*

French Knot, *page 70*

Alphabet continued
with Forget-me-nots and Violets

Forget-me-nots and violets belong to the family of "romantic flowers." They have been associated throughout the ages with innocent young love. These sweet little flowers are made using French Knots. The illustrated floral motif is a conglomeration of the floral designs used to decorate the alphabet on this and the previous pages.

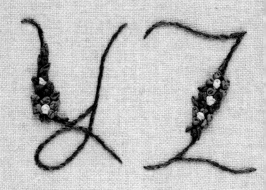

YOU WILL NEED

Fabric

Linen
10 x 12 in.
(25 x 31cm)

Needles

Assorted tapestry needles,
sizes 18 to 24

Embroidery thread

Green

Silk ribbon

Medium blue 4mm

Purple 4mm

Medium yellow 4mm

Green 4mm

PATTERN GUIDE

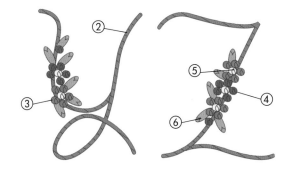

ORDER OF WORK

1. Stretch the fabric on a hoop. Transfer pattern to fabric.

Letter
2. Outline using three strands of green thread and Stem Stitch.

Forget-me-nots
3. Work five French Knots in a circle using medium blue 4mm ribbon.

Violets
4. Work five French Knots in a circle using purple 4mm ribbon.

Centers
5. Work a single French Knot using medium yellow 4mm ribbon.

Leaves
6. Work in green 4mm ribbon using Ribbon Stitch.

KEY TO STITCHES USED

Stem Stitch, *page 94*

French Knot, *page 70*

 Ribbon Stitch, *page 63*

Gathered Rose

This lovely three-dimensional rose will add richness and texture to any design. The petals of the rose are gathered and then attached with needle and thread to the background fabric. The center of the rose may be formed by stitching clusters of French Knots or one large Colonial Knot.

YOU WILL NEED

Fabric

Pure silk dupioni
10 x 12 in.
(25 x 31cm)

Needles

Chenille needles,
sizes 10 and 22

Embroidery thread

Old gold

Olive green

Silk ribbon

Olive green 2mm

Variegated green 4mm

Old gold 7mm

Variegated green 7mm

Variegated pink 7mm

Variegated pink 13mm

ORDER OF WORK

① Stretch the fabric on a hoop. Transfer pattern to fabric.

Stems

② Work using one strand of olive green thread and Stem Stitch, adding extra rows at the base of the stems. Add small Straight Stitches to represent thorns.

Grass blades

③ Work using olive green 2mm ribbon and Straight Stitch.

Small leaves

④ Work using variegated green 4mm ribbon and Ribbon Stitch.

Grass heads

⑤ Work using one strand of old gold thread and Straight Stitch.

Leaves of the large rose

⑥ Leaving room for the gathered petals, work three Detached Chain Stitches using variegated green 7mm ribbon.

Buds

⑦ Work using variegated pink 7mm ribbon and Ribbon Stitch. The center stitch of the example was padded.

Details

⑧ Using variegated green 4mm ribbon, work three Ribbon Stitches at the base of each bud and a small

PATTERN GUIDE

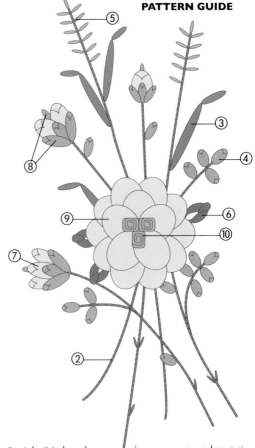

Straight Stitch at the tip of each bud.

Large rose

⑨ Gather about 18 in. (45cm) of variegated pink 13mm ribbon to make 15 petals. Starting at the outside edge, stitch down in a circle, pinning as you go to

prevent petals twisting. (*For similar gathering stitch techniques, see Gathered Ribbon Leaf, page 90, Pansy, page 96, and Cattail, page 108*).

Center of large rose

⑩ Work three Colonial Knots in old gold 7mm ribbon.

KEY TO STITCHES USED

~~~~~ Stem Stitch, *page 94*

⬬ Straight Stitch, *page 58*

⬬ Ribbon Stitch, *page 63*

◗ Detached Chain Stitch, *page 65*

▣ Colonial Knot, *page 69*

Roses and Cupids

YOU WILL NEED

Fabric

Pure silk dupioni
11¾ x 11¾ in.
(30 x 30cm)

Beads, metallic threads, jewellery findings, and charms have always been used in ribbon embroidery to add sparkle and a sense of luxury. This design has been expertly and subtly enhanced with cupid charms, and decorative threads and beads.

Needles

Chenille needle, size 18

Beading needle

Embroidery thread

Gold metallic

Silk ribbon

Light peach 4mm

Lilac 4mm

Light fawn 4mm

Light yellow 4mm

Light green 4mm

Beads

2 cupid charms

Small pink beads

Small old gold beads

PATTERN GUIDE

ORDER OF WORK

(1) Stretch the fabric on a hoop. Transfer pattern to fabric.

Flowers

(2) Work five Spider Web Roses where indicated using light peach 4mm ribbon.

(3) Work the other five-petaled flowers using Looped Straight Stitches for each of their petals. Work three using lilac 4mm ribbon and two using light fawn 4mm ribbon. Complete each flower with a Colonial Knot in the center using light yellow 4mm ribbon.

Leaves

(4) Work leaves around all the flowers in Ribbon Stitch using light green 4mm ribbon.

Decorations

(5) Fix the cupid charms on each side of the garland with the gold thread. Conceal the top of the charm with a small bow worked in lilac 4mm ribbon.

(6) Place small flowers using groups of six beads around the garland. Use one bead for each center and five for the surrounding petals. Use alternating colors of pink and old gold beads.

(7) To add sparkle, add groups of two or three extended French Knots, using one strand of gold metallic thread, around the design.

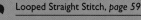

Rose Bowl

This attractive motif could be worked alone or
combined with additional stitches to create a
more complex design. The basket is worked
in Straight Stitch and the roses are made using
Colonial Knots in a variety of colored ribbons.

YOU WILL NEED

Fabric

Linen
10 x 12 in.
(25 x 31cm)

Needles

Assorted tapestry needles,
sizes 18 to 24

Silk ribbon

Dark pink 4mm

Medium pink 4mm

Light pink 4mm

Medium yellow 4mm

Cream 4mm

Green 4mm

Variegated mocha 7mm

PATTERN GUIDE

ORDER OF WORK

① Stretch the fabric on a hoop. Transfer pattern to fabric.

Basket

② Work using variegated mocha 7mm ribbon and long Straight Stitch. Ensure that the ribbon curls as it is pulled through to the back to add dimension.

Roses

③ Scatter Colonial Knot Roses (also known as Floribunda Roses) above the basket as shown using various colors of 4mm ribbon, until the area is covered.

Buds

④ Work small Straight Stitches in various colors of 4mm ribbon around the perimeter to represent buds.

Leaves

⑤ Starting at the basket and working to the top, fill all the spaces between the roses using green 4mm ribbon and small Straight Stitches.

KEY TO STITCHES USED

Straight Stitch, *page 58*

Colonial Knot, *page 69*

Butterflies of Australia

YOU WILL NEED

Fabric

Pure silk
11¾ x 11¾ in.
(30 x 30cm)

Needles

Embroidery needle, size 8

Chenille needles,
sizes 18 and 20

Beading needle

Embroidery thread

Gold metallic

Dark brown

Silk ribbon

Turquoise blue 4mm

Variegated yellow 4mm

Variegated red 4mm

Variegated pink 4mm

Variegated purple 4mm

Variegated green 4mm

Blue 4mm

White 4mm

Pink-rust 4mm

Beads

6 to 8 small white seed beads

1 larger white bead

6 to 8 small dark red seed beads

1 larger dark red bead

6 to 8 small iridescent blue seed beads

1 larger iridescent blue bead

Basic ribbon embroidery stitches may be adapted to illustrate specific flowers, insects, and images that are native, or peculiar to, a particular country or culture. In this example, Straight Stitch, Back Stitch, and Whipped Back Stitch have been used to create three butterflies found in Western Australia.

KEY TO STITCHES USED

Back Stitch, *page 126*

Straight Stitch, *page 58*

Fly Stitch *page 62*

ORDER OF WORK

1. Stretch the fabric on a hoop. Transfer pattern to fabric.

Outline

2. Work outline of all butterflies in a tiny Back Stitch using two strands of dark brown thread. Whip the Back Stitch (*similar to Whipped Chain Stitch, page 122*) using one strand of gold metallic thread.

Northern Jezabel

3. Using white 4mm ribbon, fill each panel of the wings with small Straight Stitches.
4. Work small Fly Stitches over the wings for veins.
5. Using one strand of gold metallic thread, attach small white seed beads for the body. Use a larger bead for the head.
6. Work two extended French Knots for the antennae in gold metallic thread.

Australian Beak

7. Work as for Northern Jezabel using blue 4mm ribbon for the upper wings, and pink-rust 4mm ribbon for the lower wings. Work the Fly Stitch over the wings in the gold metallic thread. Use dark red beads for the body and head.
8. For the antennae, work two extended French Knots using one strand of gold metallic thread and one strand of dark brown thread together.

PATTERN GUIDE

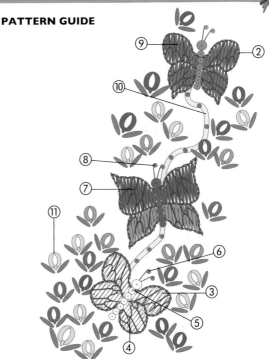

Oakblue

9. Use the turquoise blue 4mm ribbon. Work the Fly Stitch in one strand of the dark brown thread. Use iridescent blue beads for the body and head, and work the antennae as for the Australian Beak.

Stem and flowers

10. Bring the turquoise 4mm ribbon through the work just above the Northern Jezabel. Allow the ribbon to twist, and Couch it with tiny French Knots in gold metallic thread. Take the ribbon through the work at the Australian Beak and fasten at the back. Bring the ribbon up again above the Australian Beak, Couching again with French Knots and gold metallic thread, and take it back down at the tail of the Oakblue.

11. Place flowers around the design using Tête-de-boeuf Stitch and a selection of the variegated yellow, red, pink, and purple 4mm ribbons. Work the small stitches at the base in the variegated green 4mm ribbon.

Extended French Knot, *page 70*	Detached Chain Stitch, *page 65*
Couching, *page 85*	Tête-de-boeuf Stitch, *page 134*
French Knot, *page 70*	

Flower Border

This is another excellent example
illustrating the versatility of the
Scrunched Gathered Flower technique.
The flowers are all stitched in 4mm
ribbon and are further embellished
with other embroidery stitches using
stranded threads.

YOU WILL NEED

Fabric

Pure silk
11¾ x 11¾ in.
(30 x 30cm)

Needles

Fine embroidery needle

Tapestry needle,
size 24

Embroidery thread

Pale willow green

Dark willow green

Cream white

Old gold

China blue

Bark brown

White perle thread, no. 8

Silk ribbon

Pale mauve 4mm

Medium mauve 4mm

Dark mauve 4mm

Yellow 4mm

Cream 4mm

ORDER OF WORK

① Stretch the fabric on a hoop. Transfer pattern to fabric.

Tall flowers

② Form the tall flowers with Scrunched Gathered Flowers, one above the other. Make four using cream 4mm ribbon and three using yellow 4mm ribbon.

③ Add French Knots around each flower using one strand of matching thread (either yellow or cream). Also add small Straight Stitches using one strand of dark willow green thread to suggest leaves.

Mauve flowers

④ Work the flowers below the tall flowers, forming each of the five petals with Scrunched Gathered Flowers. Make two flowers using pale mauve 4mm ribbon, two in medium mauve, and two in dark mauve.

⑤ Fill the centers with French Knots using four strands of the old gold thread.

Daisies

⑥ Work three French Knots for each daisy center using four strands of old gold thread.

⑦ Work the petals using white perle thread and Straight Stitches.

PATTERN GUIDE

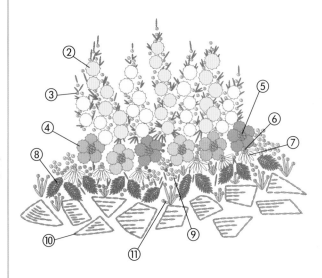

Leaves

⑧ Work the central vein using dark willow green thread and Back Stitch. Then, using the same thread, work Straight Stitches at a sharp angle along each side of the vein.

Small blue flowers

⑨ For each of the small blue flowers, work five French Knots in a circle using four strands of the China blue thread. Complete with a French Knot center in four strands of old gold thread.

Paving

⑩ Outline each of the paving slabs using one strand of bark brown thread and Back Stitch. Shade with short rows of Back Stitch.

Foliage

⑪ Fill any gaps in the design with French Knots and Straight Stitches in pale willow green.

KEY TO STITCHES USED

 Scrunched Gathered Flower, *page 93*

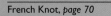 French Knot, *page 70*

 Straight Stitch, *page 58*

Back Stitch, *page 126*

Grape Arbor

A creative motif that would provide a satisfying
project for the intermediate embroidery enthusiast.
The design is visually pleasing in its simplicity and
the well-planned image perfectly captures a quiet
moment in a summer garden.

YOU WILL NEED

Fabric

Linen
10 x 12 in.
(25 x 31cm)

Needles

Assorted tapestry needles,
sizes 18 to 24

Embroidery thread

Brown

Purple

Silk ribbon

Dark brown 4mm

Purple 4mm

Gray 4mm

Light green 4mm

Dark green 4mm

Pink 4mm

Yellow 4mm

Black 4mm

Variegated cream 7mm

ORDER OF WORK

1. Stretch the fabric on a hoop. Transfer pattern to fabric.

Arbor

2. Form the arbor from three long Straight Stitches in dark brown 4mm ribbon. Couch the two sides down with one strand of brown thread. Leave the roof of the arbor uncouched.
3. Work the lattice using one strand of brown thread and long diagonal Straight Stitches in both directions.

Grapes

4. Add bunches of grapes using purple 4mm ribbon and French Knots.
5. Highlight with leaves in dark green 4mm ribbon and Straight Stitches.

Chair

6. Use Straight Stitches and dark brown 4mm ribbon to form the chair. Add the seat last to cover the ends of the vertical stitches.

Topiary

7. Work the pot using variegated cream 7mm ribbon and horizontal Straight Stitches.
8. Work the leaves in Detached Chain Stitch and light green 4mm ribbon.
9. Add roses using pink 4mm ribbon and French Knots.

PATTERN GUIDE

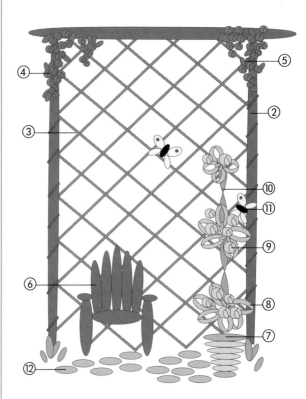

10. Form the stem of the topiary using gray 4mm ribbon and Twisted Straight Stitch.

Butterflies

11. Work the wings of the butterflies in yellow 4mm ribbon and Straight Stitch. Add spots using purple

thread and French Knots. Form the bodies with black 4mm ribbon and Straight Stitch.

Stones

12. Add stepping stones to the base of the design using gray 4mm ribbon and Straight Stitch.

KEY TO STITCHES USED

 Straight Stitch, *page 58*

Couching, *page 85*

French Knot, *page 70*

Detached Chain Stitch, *page 65*

Twisted Straight Stitch, *page 60*

Iceland Poppies

This is a three-dimensional motif created using 7mm and
13mm silk ribbon. The poppies featured here look so real
you feel that you could almost pick them off the page. The
soft, luxuriant petals are made using four gathered loop
stitches. The centers are filled with tiny black beads and
overstitched in gold embroidery thread.

YOU WILL NEED

Fabric

Pure silk
11¾ x 11¾ in.
(30 x 30cm)

Needles

Chenille needles,
sizes 16 and 18

Crewel needle, size 8

Fine embroidery needle

Beading needle

Embroidery thread

Gold (1000 denier)

Medium green

Light green

Almost pink

Fine black thread

Silk ribbon

Green 7mm

Almost pink 13mm

Beads

Tiny black seed beads

6mm bead

ORDER OF WORK

① Stretch the fabric on a hoop. Transfer pattern to fabric.

Stems

② Work stems in Whipped Chain Stitch, using medium green thread for the chain and light green to whip it with.

Flower centers

③ Fill the flower centers with tiny black seed beads, stitching through each bead twice with the fine black thread.

Leaves

④ Work the leaves in Ribbon Stitch, using green 7mm ribbon. Come back through the leaves in places and take the Ribbon Stitches off at odd angles to form the rough shape of a poppy leaf.

Petals

⑤ Each of the poppies has four overlapping petals. Using almost pink 13mm ribbon, bring the needle up through the fabric close to the center and take it back down again approximately ⅜ in. (1cm) away, again close to the center, leaving a 1 in. (3cm) loop. Fasten the ribbon at the back of the fabric. With a strand of matching almost pink embroidery thread, run a small gathering stitch along the edge of the

PATTERN GUIDE

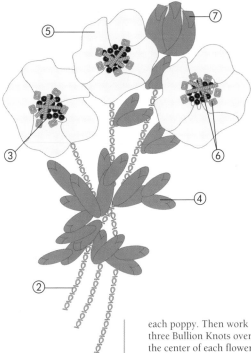

ribbon closest to the flower center. Gather up and stitch the petal to the fabric with tiny stitches almost touching the black beads. Repeat these steps for the three remaining petals, beginning each new petal approximately ¼ in. (0.5cm) over the previous stitch to form the overlap.

Stamens

⑥ Using gold 1000 denier thread, work Colonial Knots around the center of

each poppy. Then work three Bullion Knots over the center of each flower, crossing them over each other randomly.

Bud

⑦ Work a Padded Rosebud for the bud with the 6mm bead. Use almost pink 13mm ribbon for the first stitch over the bead, and green 7mm ribbon for the following stitches. When working the stitches in green ribbon, be sure to allow just a tiny bit of the pink ribbon to show through.

KEY TO STITCHES USED

 Whipped Chain Stitch, *page 122*

Ribbon Stitch, *page 63*

Colonial Knot, *page 69*

Bullion Knot, *page 127*

Padded Rosebud, *page 110*

Barcelona Mosaic

This modern motif was, as the name suggests, inspired by a visit
to Barcelona. The vibrantly colored ribbons have been worked
in gathering stitch using 7mm silk ribbons. Mosaic beads have
been added to further enhance the design.

YOU WILL NEED

Fabric

Velvet
11¾ x 11¾ in.
(30 x 30cm)

Needles

Assorted chenille needles,
sizes 13 to 26

Beading needle

Embroidery thread

Yellow

White

Red

Orange

Emerald

Royal blue

Silk ribbon

Yellow 4mm

Royal blue 4mm

White 7mm

Red 7mm

Yellow 7mm

Orange 7mm

Emerald 7mm

Beads

9 mosaic beads to match the
colors used in the design

3 long silver beads

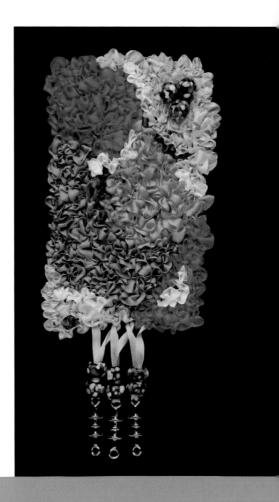

ORDER OF WORK

1. Stretch the fabric on a hoop. Transfer pattern to fabric or create your own mosaic design.

2. This design is worked using a gathering stitch as follows. Work the main blocks of color first, then fill in the gaps with the white 7mm and royal blue 4mm ribbons.

   Using thread in a matching color for each ribbon, bring the needle and thread up through the fabric and the end of the ribbon (folded under). Before taking the needle down again, gently push the ribbon back toward the entry point so that it forms a soft loop. Then, take the needle back through the ribbon and fabric, and up again.

   Work a series of Running Stitches in this way, each time pushing the ribbon back toward where the last stitch came up. As you pull the thread back through the fabric, tightening the stitch, the ribbon will take on a gathered appearance.

   The amount of ribbon you push back each time may be varied, from ¼ in. (0.5cm) for a small amount of gather to ⅜ in. (1cm) for more. The design is random within the illustrated blocks of color.

PATTERN GUIDE

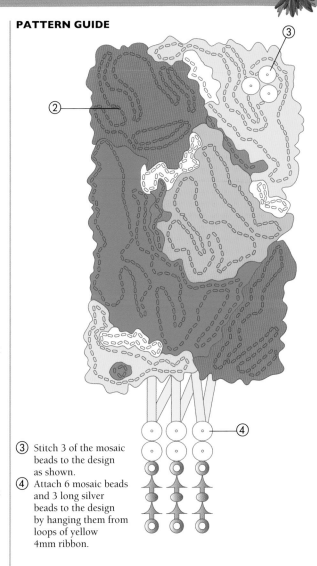

3. Stitch 3 of the mosaic beads to the design as shown.

4. Attach 6 mosaic beads and 3 long silver beads to the design by hanging them from loops of yellow 4mm ribbon.

KEY TO STITCHES USED

Running Stitch, *page 73*

Strawberry Delight

A delicious embroidered motif certainly created
to inspire thoughts of summer. These lush, plump
strawberries and creamy butterflies would be the
perfect embroidery with which to decorate the linen
used for serving afternoon tea with scones,
strawberry jam, and lashings of cream.

YOU WILL NEED

Fabric

Linen
10 x 12 in.
(25 x 31cm)

Needles

Assorted tapestry needles,
sizes 18 to 24

Embroidery thread

Gold yellow

Black

Silk ribbon

Green 4mm

Burgundy 4mm

Brown 4mm

Red 7mm

White 7mm

Yellow 7mm

ORDER OF WORK

① Stretch the fabric on a hoop. Transfer pattern to fabric.

Strawberries

② Form each berry using three Looped Straight Stitches and red 7mm ribbon. Do the outside stitches first and then the central stitch, making sure that the central stitch slightly overlaps the outside stitches.

③ Add leaves to the berries using Looped Straight Stitches and green 4mm ribbon.

④ Form the strawberry seeds with tiny Straight Stitches in one strand of gold yellow thread.

Blossoms

⑤ Work the flower petals in Ribbon Stitch and white 7mm ribbon.

⑥ Work the centers in one Looped Straight Stitch and yellow 7mm ribbon.

Stems

⑦ Work in Twisted Straight Stitch and green 4mm ribbon.

Butterflies

⑧ Work the wings using Looped Straight Stitches and yellow 7mm ribbon.

⑨ Form the head and body with an extended French Knot in brown 4mm ribbon.

PATTERN GUIDE

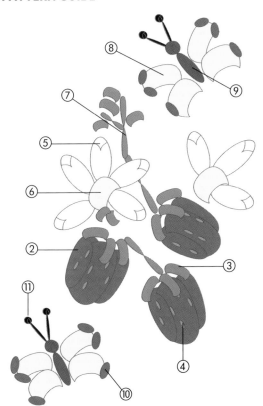

⑩ Accent the ends of the wings with Straight Stitches in burgundy 4mm ribbon.

⑪ Add antennae with extended French Knots in one strand of black thread. (The French Knots should be at the tip of the antennae.)

KEY TO STITCHES USED

Looped Straight Stitch, *page 59*

Straight Stitch, *page 58*

Ribbon Stitch, *page 63*

Twisted Straight Stitch, *page 60*

Extended French Knot, *page 70*

Twig Heart

This simple design is suitable for anything from clothing to pillows or box tops. It is ideal for a wedding when worked in white or cream, or in a color to complement the bridesmaids' dresses.

YOU WILL NEED

Fabric

Pure silk dupioni
10 x 12 in.
(25 x 31cm)

Needles

Chenille needles,
sizes 10 and 22

Beading needle

Embroidery thread

Olive green

Silk ribbon

Olive green 4mm

Pink 4mm

Yellow 4mm

Blue 4mm

Beads and trimmings

Cream seed beads

Glass or brass trinkets

PATTERN GUIDE

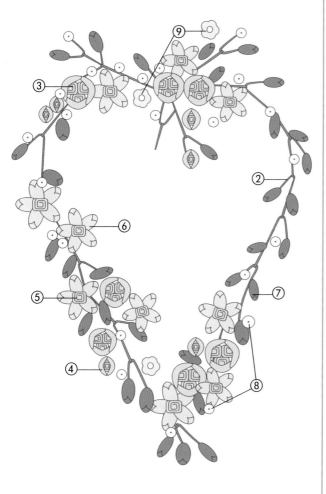

ORDER OF WORK

① Stretch the fabric on a hoop. Transfer pattern to fabric.

Heart shape
② Beginning at the base, work using one strand of olive green thread and Fly Stitch.

Rose centers
③ Work three Colonial Knots, in pink 4mm ribbon, closely together for the center of each rose. Wrap each group of knots with Straight Stitches.

Buds
④ Work a Colonial Knot in pink 4mm ribbon for each bud. Work a Straight Stitch on either side to cup the knot.

Blue flower centers
⑤ Work using yellow 4mm ribbon and Colonial Knots.

Petals
⑥ Work in blue 4mm ribbon using Ribbon Stitch.

Leaves
⑦ Work leaves along the vine using olive green 4mm ribbon and Ribbon Stitch.

Details
⑧ Scatter cream seed beads among the leaves.
⑨ Add glass or brass trinkets if desired.

KEY TO STITCHES USED

 Fly Stitch, *page 62*

Colonial Knot, *page 69*

Straight Stitch, *page 58*

Ribbon Stitch, *page 63*

Swag of Ribbon Flowers

YOU WILL NEED

Fabric

Pure silk dupioni
11¾ x 11¾ in.
(30 x 30cm)

Needles

Fine embroidery needle

Tapestry needle, size 24

Embroidery thread

Pale willow green

Dark willow green

Apple green

Old gold

Plum

Golden brown

Silk ribbon

Dark pink 4mm

Pale pink 4mm

Yellow 4mm

Cream 4mm

The Scrunched Gathered Flowers and Spider Web Roses worked in this design are all stitched in 4mm ribbon. French Knots are used to create the delicate flower sprays, and the leaves and ferns are stitched in stranded embroidery thread.

KEY TO STITCHES USED

 Scrunched Gathered Flower, *page 93*

French Knot, *page 70*

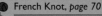 Spider Web Rose, *page 112*

PATTERN GUIDE

ORDER OF WORK

① Stretch the fabric on a hoop. Transfer pattern to fabric.

Flowers

② Work three yellow and two cream flowers forming the five petals of each with Scrunched Gathered Flowers. Use the yellow 4mm and the cream 4mm ribbons.

③ Fill the centers with French Knots worked in four strands of old gold thread.

④ Work two pale pink and two dark pink Spider Web Roses where indicated, using two strands of the golden brown thread to form the spokes of each rose, and the pale pink and dark pink 4mm ribbons for the weaving.

⑤ Work the small flowers in French Knots and four strands of plum thread. Add Straight Stitches around them in pale willow green to suggest the stems and foliage.

Ferns and foliage

⑥ Back Stitch the stems of the ferns in one strand of apple green thread and add Straight Stitches at sharp angles along the stem.

⑦ Outline each of the large leaves and work the central vein using two strands of dark willow green thread and Split Stitch. Use Shaded Satin Stitch to fill the leaves, using one strand of dark willow green thread for the outer stitches and one strand of pale willow green thread for the center stitches.

⑧ Add fans of Straight Stitches in one strand of dark willow green thread in the gaps between the flowers.

Straight Stitch, *page 58*

Back Stitch, *page 126*

Split Stitch, *page 126*

Shaded Satin Stitch, *page 128*

Summer Day

A fun design that, if stitched for a gift card, would suit a number of different occasions including birthdays and thank-you notes. Stitch and frame it as illustrated, or use it as a focal point for developing a more elaborate design.

YOU WILL NEED

Fabric

Linen
10 x 12 in.
(25 x 31cm)

Needles

Assorted tapestry needles, sizes 18 to 24

Embroidery thread

Black

Gold yellow

Silk ribbon

Gray 4mm

Black 4mm

Dark red 4mm

Dark brown 4mm

Medium green 4mm

Variegated cream 7mm

Dark green 7mm

ORDER OF WORK

(1) Stretch the fabric on a hoop. Transfer pattern to fabric.

Fence

(2) Work the fence posts using Split Stitch and variegated cream 7mm ribbon.

(3) Form the rails using the same ribbon and a long Twisted Straight Stitch.

Birdbath

(4) Using gray 4mm ribbon and Straight Stitch, work the stand of the birdbath (two long stitches), followed by the base and bowl.

Spider web

(5) Work the spider web using one strand of black thread and long Straight Stitches.

(6) Form the body of the spider with a French Knot in black 4mm ribbon. Work the legs in one strand of black thread and Straight Stitches.

Cardinals

(7) Using dark red 7mm ribbon, create the cardinals with one large French Knot (two wraps) for the body, a smaller French Knot for the head, and a short Straight Stitch for the tail.

(8) The beaks are formed using gold yellow thread and two small Straight Stitches in a V-shape.

PATTERN GUIDE

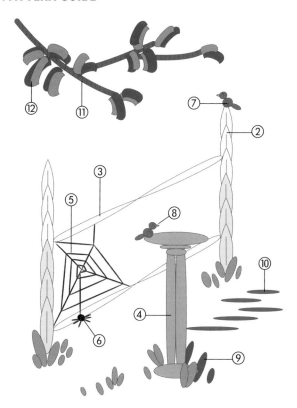

Grass and steps

(9) Work the grass in medium green 4mm ribbon and Straight Stitch.

(10) Work the steps in dark brown 4mm ribbon and Straight Stitch.

Branch

(11) Using Stem Stitch and dark brown 4mm ribbon, work the overhanging branch.

(12) Add leaves in dark green 7mm ribbon and Looped Straight Stitch. Work a second layer of leaves in medium green 4mm ribbon and Looped Straight Stitch for contrast.

KEY TO STITCHES USED

Split Stitch, *page 126*

Twisted Straight Stitch, *page 60*

Straight Stitch, *page 58*

French Knot, *page 70*

Stem Stitch, *page 94*

Looped Straight Stitch, *page 59*

Weeping Willow Garden

This motif could be worked alone and framed, or, for the adventurous embroiderer, used as the basis for a more ambitious project. Consider combining elements from this design with motifs such as *Grape Arbor* on page 208 or *Summer Day* on page 220.

YOU WILL NEED

Fabric

Linen
10 x 12 in.
(25 x 31cm)

Needles

Assorted tapestry needles, sizes 18 to 24

Embroidery thread

Gold yellow

Black

Silk ribbon

Dark brown 4mm

Dark green 4mm

Medium green 4mm

Light green 4mm

White 4mm

Bright blue 4mm

Gray 4mm

Red 7mm

ORDER OF WORK

① Stretch the fabric on a hoop. Transfer pattern to fabric.

Tree

② Work the trunk and main branches in dark brown 4mm ribbon and Stem Stitch.

③ Form the drooping boughs and leaves with long Twisted Straight Stitches and the dark, medium, and light green 4mm ribbons. Alternate the colors and the lengths of the stitches for a more natural look.

Bench

④ Work the bench in white 4mm ribbon and Straight Stitches. Do the seat last to cover the ends of the vertical stitches.

Birdhouse

⑤ Work the pole in gray 4mm ribbon and one long Straight Stitch.

⑥ Work the house using red 7mm ribbon and one Straight Stitch. The base and roof of the house are made with Straight Stitches and dark brown 4mm ribbon. The entrance is one French Knot in black embroidery thread.

Bluebirds

⑦ Work the bodies in bright blue 4mm ribbon and a large French Knot (two wraps). The heads are a smaller French Knot (one wrap). Work the tails in a short Straight Stitch.

PATTERN GUIDE

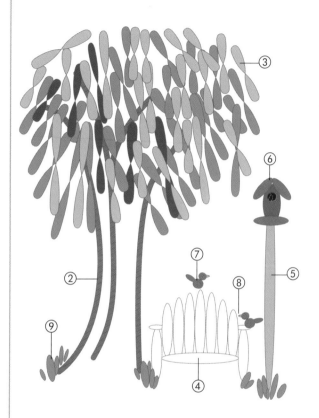

⑧ The beaks are formed using gold yellow thread and two small Straight Stitches in a V-shape.

Grass

⑨ Add grass where desired using medium green 4mm ribbon and Straight Stitches.

KEY TO STITCHES USED

Stem Stitch, *page 94*	Straight Stitch, *page 58*
Twisted Straight Stitch, *page 60*	French Knot, *page 70*

Victorian Tree

This holiday motif would work well as a decoration on Christmas stockings, greeting cards, or festive table linen. Create miniature trees by reducing the size of the pattern and using 2 or 4mm ribbons.

YOU WILL NEED

Fabric

Linen
10 x 12 in.
(25 x 31cm)

Needles

Assorted tapestry needles, sizes 18 to 24

Beading needle

Embroidery thread

Gold metallic

Invisible (optional)

Silk ribbon

Red 4mm

Dark green 7mm

White 7mm

Beads

Small red bugle beads

Small gold glass beads

ORDER OF WORK

① Stretch the fabric on a hoop. Transfer pattern to fabric.

Tree

② Using a long Ribbon Stitch and beginning at the bottom of the tree, work the tree in dark green 7mm ribbon. Stagger each row between the previous row, reducing each row by one stitch until you reach the top. Add further Ribbon Stitches to fill any gaps.

Star

③ Place a star at the top of the tree using Star Stitch and two strands of gold metallic thread. Continue down the tree to form the gold garland by coming up on the left side, twisting the thread, and going back into the fabric on the right. Work to the bottom of the tree.

Ornaments and gifts

④ Scatter French Knots in red 4mm ribbon.
⑤ Place candles at the tips of the boughs (just above the curl of the Ribbon Stitch) by fastening a red bugle bead with either gold metallic or invisible thread. Then stitch a small gold bead above the bugle bead.
⑥ Work the gifts below the tree using Straight Stitch and white 7mm ribbon.

PATTERN GUIDE

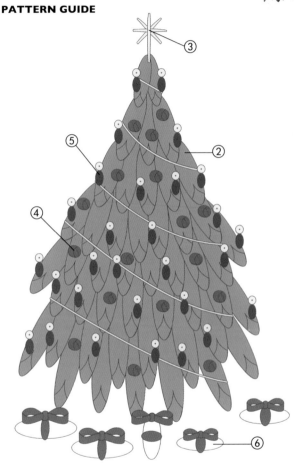

Place another Straight Stitch in red 4mm ribbon crosswise over the top of the white ribbon and finish with a Loop Stitch Bow.

KEY TO STITCHES USED

Ribbon Stitch, *page 63*

Star Stitch, *page 86*

French Knot, *page 70*

Straight Stitch, *page 58*

Loop Stitch Bow, *page 67*

225

Chrysanthemum

This beautifully stitched exotic flower has
been worked in hand-dyed silk ribbon and
embroidery silk. The two strands of
embroidery silk create an excellent textural
contrast with the voluminous head of the
flower and buds. Some time and care must
be taken to achieve similar results.

YOU WILL NEED

Fabric

Pure silk dupioni
15 x 15 in.
(38 x 38cm)

Felt to match flower
ribbon or fabric
2 x 2 in.
(5 x 5cm)

Needles

Chenille needle, size 22

Crewel needle, size 5

Embroidery thread

Green

Silk ribbon

Variegated blue-gray 4mm

Medium mauve 4mm

Green-gold 4mm

Old gold 4mm

ORDER OF WORK

1. Stretch the fabric on a hoop. Transfer pattern to fabric.

Bud padding

2. Cut one felt shape of each size for each bud. Place the larger shape over the smaller and stitch to fabric.

Stems

3. Work using one strand of green thread and Whipped Chain Stitch.

Leaves

4. Using one strand of green thread, start each leaf with a Straight Stitch. Complete in Fly Stitch, working stitches very close together.

Petals

5. Work the first layer using medium mauve 4mm ribbon and a mixture of loose Straight and Twisted Straight Stitches.

6. Work a second layer in the same way, using variegated blue-gray 4mm ribbon but making the stitches a little looser and fuller for a more three-dimensional effect.

Buds

7. Using variegated blue-gray 4mm ribbon and Ribbon Stitch, work the buds over the felt padding. Work some stitches through the ribbon already in place and the padding itself.

PATTERN GUIDE

2 Padding layers

Calyx

8. Work using green-gold 4mm ribbon and Ribbon Stitch, going through previous stitches and padding.

Flower center

9. Using the old gold and green-gold 4mm ribbons, fill with French Knots.

KEY TO STITCHES USED

Whipped Chain Stitch, *page 122*	Twisted Straight Stitch, *page 60*
Straight Stitch, *page 58*	Ribbon Stitch, *page 63*
Fly Stitch, *page 62*	French Knot, *page 70*

Flower Triangle

The background triangles are made with gold metallic thread and the Couching technique. They form an interesting border pattern that contrasts nicely with the more traditional floral embroidery.

YOU WILL NEED

Fabric

Pure silk dupioni
11¾ x 11¾ in.
(30 x 30cm)

Needles

Fine embroidery needle

Tapestry needle, size 24

Embroidery thread

Dark willow green

Apple green

Old gold

Plum

Golden brown

Gold metallic

Silk ribbon

Dark mauve 4mm

Medium mauve 4mm

Yellow 4mm

Cream 4mm

Lemon yellow 4mm

PATTERN GUIDE

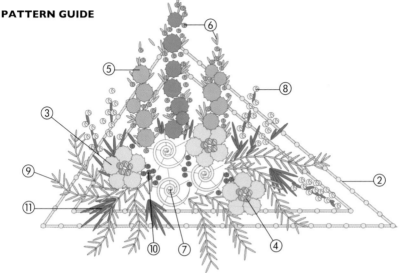

ORDER OF WORK

(1) Stretch the fabric on a hoop. Transfer pattern to fabric.

Triangle

(2) Couch two strands of the gold metallic thread around the outer triangle outline. Couch a second triangle within the first about ¼ in. (0.5cm) away.

Flowers

(3) Work three yellow flowers forming each of the five petals with a Scrunched Gathered Flower. Use the yellow 4mm ribbon.

(4) Fill the centers with French Knots using two strands of old gold thread and one strand of plum.

(5) Work Scrunched Gathered Flowers one above the other to form the tall flowers. The central tall flower is worked in dark mauve 4mm ribbon and the two side flowers in medium mauve.

(6) Use one strand of the plum thread to work French Knots around the tall flowers. Add Straight Stitches in two strands of apple green thread to suggest leaves.

(7) Work three Spider Web Roses, two in lemon yellow 4mm and one in cream 4mm ribbon. Use two strands of the golden brown thread to work the spokes of the Spider Web Roses.

(8) Work smaller flowers in French Knots using four strands of golden brown thread. Add Straight Stitches around them in dark willow green thread to suggest stems and leaves.

Ferns and foliage

(9) Work the fern stems in Back Stitch and one strand of apple green thread. Add Straight Stitches at sharp angles along the stems.

(10) Work French Knots in dark willow green thread in any gaps between the flowers.

(11) Add fans of Straight Stitches in dark willow green thread to suggest additional foliage.

KEY TO STITCHES USED

 Couching, *page 85*

Scrunched Gathered Flower, *page 93*

 French Knot, *page 70*

Straight Stitch, *page 58*

Spider Web Rose, *page 112*

Back Stitch, *page 126*

Spider Chrysanthemum

The spider chrysanthemum flower motif is created using Twisted Straight Stitches. This natural, life-like image is enhanced by loosening the gauge on the outside petal stitches. This image would work well as pillow or curtain embroidery and would combine well with the chrysanthemum motif on page 226.

YOU WILL NEED

Fabric

Pure silk dupioni
15 x 15 in.
(38 x 38cm)

Needles

Chenille needles,
sizes 22 and 24
Crewel needle, size 5

Embroidery thread

Leaf green

Yellow

Green

Silk ribbon

White 2mm

White 4mm

Medium avocado 4mm

Light avocado 4mm

PATTERN GUIDE

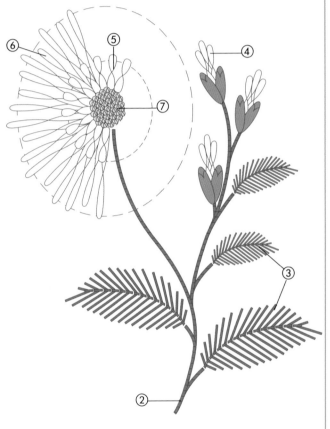

ORDER OF WORK

1. Stretch the fabric on a hoop. Transfer pattern to fabric.

Stems

2. Work using four strands of leaf green thread and Stem Stitch.

Leaves

3. Using medium avocado 4mm ribbon for the two larger leaves, and light avocado for the two smaller leaves, work in Fly Stitch.

Buds

4. Using white 2mm ribbon, work three loose Twisted Straight Stitches for each bud. Using light avocado 4mm ribbon, work a Ribbon Stitch on either side of the bud petals.

Flower petals

5. Using white 4mm ribbon, work a regular circle of loose Twisted Straight Stitches close to the center to form the first layer of petals.

6. Work a second layer of longer petals in the same way, using white 2mm ribbon. Make these stitches a little looser and slightly uneven in length.

Flower center

7. Fill with French Knots using three strands of yellow and one strand of green thread together.

KEY TO STITCHES USED

Stem Stitch, *page 94*

Fly Stitch, *page 62*

Twisted Straight Stitch, *page 60*

 Ribbon Stitch, *page 63*

 French Knot, *page 70*

Flower Garland

For the more advanced embroiderer, this motif offers a variety of techniques to experiment with. Several different ribbon and freestyle embroidery stitches are used and the finished piece has been quilted for a very elegant look.

YOU WILL NEED

Fabric

	Pure silk 11¾ x 11¾ in. (30 x 30cm)
	Batting fabric (pellon)

Needles

	Fine embroidery needle
	Tapestry needle, size 24
	Beading needle

Embroidery thread

	Pale willow green
	Dark willow green
	Apple green
	Plum
	Maize gold
	White perle thread, no. 8

Silk ribbon

	Pale pink 4mm
	Medium pink 4mm
	Dark pink 4mm
	Yellow 4mm
	Pale mauve 4mm
	Pink-mauve 4mm
	Dark mauve 4mm

Beads

	Small gold beads

KEY TO STITCHES USED

 Spider Web Rose, *page 112*

 Scrunched Gathered Flower, *page 93*

● French Knot, *page 70*

ORDER OF WORK

① Stretch the fabric on a hoop. Transfer pattern to fabric.

Roses

② Work Spider Web Roses where indicated. Make two in pale pink, two in medium pink, and one in dark pink 4mm ribbon.

Flowers

③ Work the other large, five-petaled flowers as indicated, working Scrunched Gathered Flowers for each petal. Work five in yellow 4mm ribbon, five in pale mauve, two in pink-mauve, and three in dark mauve.

④ Fill their centers with small gold beads and French Knots in four strands of maize gold thread.

⑤ Work each of the small white flowers using the white perle thread and five French Knots in a circle. Finish with a French Knot using four strands of maize gold thread in the center.

Leaves and foliage

⑥ Outline each of the large leaves and work the central vein using two strands of dark willow green thread and Split Stitch. Use Shaded Satin Stitch to fill the leaves, using one strand of dark willow green thread for the outer stitches and one

PATTERN GUIDE

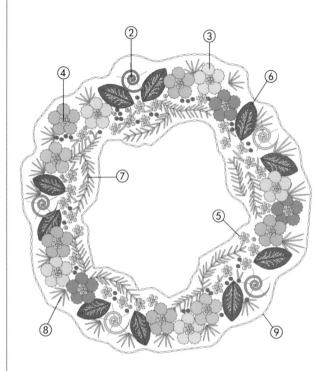

strand of pale willow green thread for the center stitches.

⑦ Work the fern stems in Back Stitch and one strand of apple green thread. Add Straight Stitches at sharp angles along the stems.

⑧ Add fans of Straight Stitches in one strand of apple green thread in any

gaps left around the design.

Quilting

⑨ Place a batting fabric, such as pellon, behind the work. Outline the design, attaching the work to the batting fabric, using Back Stitch, to create a soft quilted effect.

Split Stitch, *page 126*

Shaded Satin Stitch, *page 128*

Straight Stitch, *page 58*

 Back Stitch, *page 126*

Lavender Thyme

When using wider width ribbons it is important to consider the length of the stitch. Ideally, the stitches should be longer than the width of the ribbon being used. The stitches used in this design allow the ribbon to open fully creating texture and resulting in a well-balanced design.

YOU WILL NEED

Fabric

Moiré silk
6½ x 10 in.
(16 x 25cm)

Interfacing
6½ x 10 in.
(16 x 25cm)

Needle

Chenille needle, size 18

Embroidery thread

Green

Silk ribbon

Green 4mm

Variegated green 7mm

Variegated lavender 7mm

Sundries

Sewing thread

PATTERN GUIDE

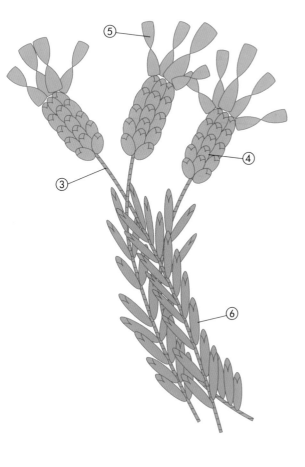

ORDER OF WORK

① Tack interfacing and moiré silk together using the sewing thread. Place in hoop and pull fabric taut.

② Transfer design to the moiré silk.

Stems

③ Work stems using green thread and Whipped Chain Stitch.

Flower heads

④ Starting at the base of each flower, work upward using green 7mm ribbon and Ribbon Stitch. Continue for about four to six rows until covered.

Petals

⑤ Add petals to the tip of each flower head using lavender 7mm ribbon and Ribbon Stitch, adding a slight twist to some.

Leaves

⑥ Work leaves up the stems using green 4mm ribbon and Ribbon Stitch.

KEY TO STITCHES USED

 Whipped Chain Stitch, page 122

Ribbon Stitch, page 63

Hearts and Flowers

This romantic motif is perfect for embellishing family heirlooms such as a baby's christening gown, wedding memorabilia, or a special anniversary gift card. It is a more complex design that calls for intermediate to advanced stitching skills.

YOU WILL NEED

Fabric

Pure silk dupioni
11¾ x 11¾ in.
(30 x 30cm)

Needle

Fine embroidery needle

Tapestry needle, size 24

Beading needle

Embroidery thread

Dark willow green

Apple green

Variegated rose

Maize gold

Lemon yellow

White perle thread, no. 8

Gold metallic

Silk ribbon

Pale pink 4mm

Medium pink 4mm

Dark pink 4mm

Yellow 4mm

Cream 4mm

Beads

Small gold beads

KEY TO STITCHES USED

 Spider Web Rose, *page 112*

 Scrunched Gathered Flower, *page 93*

French Knot, *page 70*

ORDER OF WORK

① Stretch the fabric on a hoop. Transfer pattern to fabric.

Roses

② Work Spider Web Roses where indicated. Make three using cream 4mm ribbon and two using yellow 4mm ribbon.

Flowers

③ Work the five flowers at the top of the design using a Scrunched Gathered Flower for each of their five petals. Work two using dark pink 4mm ribbon, two in medium pink, and one in pale pink.

④ Fill their centers with French Knots in four strands of either maize gold or lemon yellow thread.

Heart outline

⑤ Outline the heart with two strands of gold metallic thread, Couched to the fabric. Add a second outline within the first about ¼ in. (0.5cm) away in the same manner.

⑥ Stitch a row of small gold beads between the two rows of gold metallic thread.

Bow

⑦ Outline the bow with Split Stitch using variegated rose thread. Then work Satin Stitch over the outline using the same thread.

PATTERN GUIDE

Daisies

⑧ Work three French Knots in four strands of maize gold thread for the centers of each daisy.

⑨ Work the petals in Straight Stitch and white perle thread.

Ferns and foliage

⑩ Work the fern stems in Back Stitch using one strand of apple green thread. Add Straight Stitches at a sharp angle on either side of the stems in the same thread.

⑪ Add fans of Straight Stitches using one strand of apple green thread in any gaps between the roses and between each of the flowers at the top of the design.

⑫ Using four strands of apple green thread, stitch French Knots between the flowers at the top and the heart.

 Couching, page 85

Split Stitch, page 126

Satin Stitch, page 84

Straight Stitch, page 58

Back Stitch, page 126

Ribbon Bouquet

This motif demands expert ribbon handling and stitching techniques. Although the stitches used to create the design are not difficult to master, and feature in less complicated designs such as *Swag of Ribbon Flowers* on page 218 and *Flower Triangle* on page 228, a novice or intermediate stitcher may wish to practice with these earlier designs before attempting this motif.

YOU WILL NEED

Fabric

Pure cotton
9 x 11 in.
(23 x 28cm)

Needles

Fine embroidery needle

Tapestry needle, no. 24

Silk embroidery thread

Orange yellow

Cream white

Rose

Plum

Pale willow green

Medium willow green

Dark willow green

Silk ribbon

Medium pink 4mm

Apple green 4mm

Dark mauve 4mm

Medium mauve 4mm

Pale mauve 4mm

White 4mm

Buttercup yellow 4mm

KEY TO STITCHES USED

 Spider Web Rose, *page 112*

Scrunched Gathered Flower, *page 93*

 French Knot, *page 70*

ORDER OF WORK

① Stretch the fabric on a hoop. Transfer pattern to fabric.

Roses

② Using medium pink 4mm ribbon, work three Spider Web Roses. Use two strands of the rose thread for the spokes of the roses.

Gathered flowers

③ Work the three flowers in pale mauve, medium mauve, and dark mauve 4mm ribbon. Each of their seven petals should be one Scrunched Gathered Flower. Fill centers with a mixture of French Knots.

Tall flowers

④ Work Scrunched Gathered Flowers, one above the other. Use white 4mm ribbon for the central flower and buttercup yellow 4mm ribbon for the flowers at either side. Work French Knots in the spaces between.

⑤ Work Straight Stitches around the flowers, using one strand of pale willow green thread around the central flower and one strand of medium willow green thread around the flowers at each side.

Ferns and leaves

⑥ Work the stems in a row of Back Stitch and Straight Stitches.

⑦ Outline each of the large leaves and work the central vein using two strands of

PATTERN GUIDE

dark willow green thread and Split Stitch. Use Shaded Satin Stitch to fill the leaves, using dark willow green thread for the outer stitches and one strand of pale willow green thread for the center stitches.

Daisies

⑧ Work three French Knots in two strands of orange yellow thread for each daisy center. Work the petals using two strands of

cream white thread and Straight Stitches.

Other flowers and foliage

⑨ Work leaves around the design using apple green ribbon and Straight Stitch.

⑩ Work flowers made with five French Knot petals in a circle using four strands of plum thread. Add another French Knot using four strands of orange yellow thread for the center of each flower.

Back Stitch, *page 126*

Split Stitch, *page 126*

Shaded Satin Stitch, *page 128*

Straight Stitch, *page 58*

Lilac in Springtime

This motif is an exciting new concept in silk ribbon.
Felt shapes are couched to the background fabric
using Buttonhole Stitch. The felt works as a padding
for the ribbons that are later stitched to it. The ribbon
is treated with PVA glue and allowed to dry and stiffen.
Petal shapes are cut from the ribbon and then stitched
to the felt, creating a highly textured effect.

YOU WILL NEED

Fabric
Moiré silk
6½ x 10 in. (16 x 25cm)

Interfacing
6½ x 10 in. (16 x 25cm)

Purple felt
4 x 4 in. (10 x 10cm)

Needles
Embroidery needle, size 10

Tapestry needle, size 22

Embroidery thread
Purple

Light brown

Green

Tapestry thread
Brown

Silk ribbon
Purple 7mm

Green 1 in. (25mm)

Sundries
PVA craft adhesive

Double-sided bonding web

Sewing thread

ORDER OF WORK

① Tack interfacing and moiré silk together using the sewing thread. Place in hoop and pull fabric taut.

② Transfer padding layers design to bonding web and iron the web onto the felt. Cut out the three shapes.

③ Transfer design to moiré silk. Starting with the smallest, couch the felt shapes in place in layers using purple thread. Work Buttonhole Stitch around the top layer of felt to seal edge.

Stem

④ Lay long Straight Stitches of brown tapestry thread until stem area is covered. Couch these at ⅛ in. (3mm) intervals using light brown thread. Work rows of raised Stem Stitch over the top until the tapestry thread is covered.

Making the petals

⑤ Set aside 8 in. (20cm) purple 7mm ribbon. Mix one teaspoonful of PVA adhesive and half a cup of water. Run ribbon through mix, then remove excess. Place one end of ribbon on table edge. Leave to dry and stiffen.

⑥ Fold ribbon in half lengthwise. With the folded edge as the base

PATTERN GUIDE

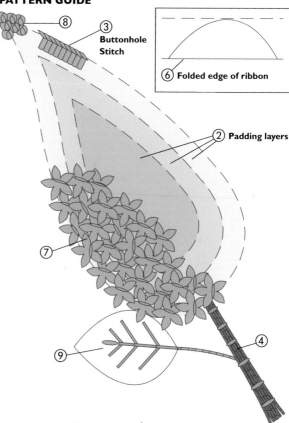

Buttonhole Stitch

⑥ **Folded edge of ribbon**

② **Padding layers**

cut out petal shapes (see enlarged pattern above). They need not all be the same size.

Attaching petals

⑦ Arrange groups of four or five petals on the felt. Place small ⅛ in. (3mm) Straight Stitches into the base of each petal. Continue until the felt padding is covered.

Buds

⑧ Add a few French Knots using purple 7mm ribbon to the top of flower to represent buds.

Leaves

⑨ Cut leaf shapes from green 1 in. (25mm) ribbon. Work Fly Stitch in green thread down leaf toward stem.

KEY TO STITCHES USED

Buttonhole Stitch, *page 123*

Straight Stitch, *page 58*

Stem Stitch, *page 94*

French Knot, *page 70*

Fly Stitch, *page 62*

Pom Pom Chrysanthemum

The bright heads of the chrysanthemum flowers illustrated here almost burst off the background fabric. This is an exciting and unusual use of Looped Straight Stitch. To create even and perfectly formed loops, use a chopstick to support and control the ribbon as the stitch is being formed.

YOU WILL NEED

Fabric

Pure silk dupioni
10 x 12 in.
(25 x 31cm)

Felt to match flower
ribbon or fabric
4 x 4 in.
(10 x 10cm)

Needles

Chenille needles,
sizes 18 and 22
Crewel needle, size 5

Embroidery thread

Green

Silk ribbon

Light leaf green 4mm

Cerise 4mm

Cerise 7mm

PATTERN GUIDE

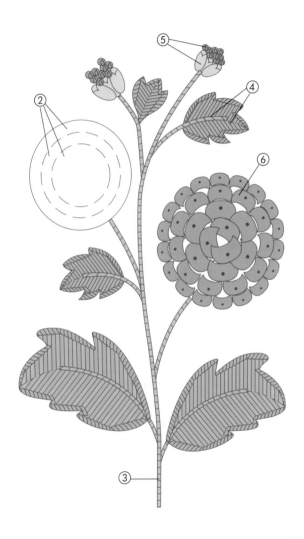

ORDER OF WORK

① Stretch the fabric on a hoop. Transfer pattern to fabric.

Felt padding

② Following the guide, cut a felt circle for each flower. Cut two more circles for each flower, each slightly smaller than the one before. Stack one on top of the other, beginning with the smallest. Stitch in place.

Stems

③ Work in Stem Stitch using one or two strands of green thread.

Leaves

④ Work using green thread and Buttonhole Stitch. Work the center vein in Stem Stitch.

Buds

⑤ Fill the tops of the buds using cerise 4mm ribbon and French Knots. Work the calyx using light leaf green 4mm ribbon and Ribbon Stitch.

Flower heads

⑥ Using cerise 7mm ribbon, work Looped Straight Stitch through all the layers of padding. Fill the middle third of the flower head with 7–8mm loops, and the rest with 4–5mm loops.

KEY TO STITCHES USED

Stem Stitch, page 94

Buttonhole Stitch, page 123

Ribbon Stitch, page 63

French Knot, page 70

Looped Straight Stitch, page 59

Country Garden

This design cannot fail to inspire every embroidery enthusiast. The motif is meticulously planned with foreground, middle distance, and background all suggested through the size of the stitches and the careful attention to detail.

YOU WILL NEED

Fabric

	Pure cotton 9 x 11 in. (23 x 28cm)

Needles

Fine embroidery needle

Tapestry needle, no. 24

Silk embroidery thread

Pale sage green

Dark sage green

Old gold

Plum

Bark brown

Pale willow green

Cream white

Rose

China blue

Silk ribbon

Medium pink 4mm

White 4mm

Dark mauve 4mm

Medium mauve 4mm

Pale mauve 4mm

Buttercup yellow 4mm

Pale yellow 4mm

KEY TO STITCHES USED

Stem Stitch, *page 94*

Satin Stitch, *page 84*

 French Knot, *page 70*

PATTERN GUIDE

ORDER OF WORK

① Stretch the fabric on a hoop. Transfer pattern to fabric. However, do not attempt to transfer the crazy paving pattern as it will be difficult to ensure all the lines are covered.

House

② Using Stem Stitch and a single strand of bark brown thread, outline the house, bricks, doorway, and window.

③ Using a single strand of China blue thread, fill in the window panes with diagonal stitches. Stitch the door with the same thread, using Stem Stitch for the sides of the door, Satin Stitch for the bars across, and filling the panels with diagonal stitches in both directions.

Lawn

④ Use a single strand of pale willow green thread and Stem Stitch to suggest the lawn.

Distant greenery

⑤ Work the climber over the door and the greenery under the window in French Knots, using four strands of embroidery thread in each color. Use pale willow green, pale sage green, and old gold around the door, and pale willow green, rose, and plum under the window.

continued on next page

 Back Stitch, *page 126*

 Straight Stitch, *page 58*

 Scrunched Gathered Flower, *page 93*

Spider Web Rose, *page 112*

Country Garden
continued from previous page

Crazy paving

⑥ Work the crazy paving using a single strand of bark brown thread and Back Stitch. Begin with smaller shapes at the top of the path and gradually enlarge the shapes toward the lower part of the path.

Flowers at left

⑦ Work the petals of the daisies on the left using two strands of cream white thread and Straight Stitch. Finish each with a French Knot worked in four strands of old gold thread. Work foliage around the daisies using two strands of pale sage green thread and Straight Stitch.

⑧ Below the daisies, work Scrunched Gathered Flowers in medium pink and dark mauve 4mm ribbon.

⑨ Surround these with French Knots in four strands of dark sage green thread.

Flowers at right

⑩ Work Scrunched Gathered Flowers one above the other in pale yellow and buttercup yellow 4mm ribbon to create the tall flowers. Surround them with French Knots in two strands of old gold thread, and Straight Stitches in a single strand of pale sage green thread. Work fans of Straight Stitches under the flowers using a single strand of pale sage green thread.

⑪ Working down the right-hand side, stitch the next three flowers using medium pink 4mm ribbon and five French Knots in a circle. Fill the centers with French Knots using four strands of old gold thread. Surround the flowers with French Knots using four strands of dark sage green thread.

⑫ Stitch the petals of these daisies with Straight Stitches and white 4mm ribbon. Use six strands of old gold thread and French Knots to fill the centers. Create the foliage using two strands of pale sage green thread and Straight Stitches.

⑬ Below the daisies, work the five-petaled flowers where marked using pale, medium, and dark mauve 4mm ribbon; each of the five petals should be one Scrunched Gathered Flower. Fill the centers with French Knots in four strands of old gold thread. Surround the flowers with French Knots in four strands of dark sage green thread.

⑭ Work three more daisies in the right-hand corner in the same way as for 12.

⑮ Work five Spider Web Roses in the center using medium pink 4mm ribbon. Work the leaves around them using a Straight Stitch and a single strand of pale willow green thread for the central vein, followed by slanting Straight Stitches to each side of the vein.

⑯ At the bottom left, work Scrunched Gathered Flowers in buttercup yellow 4mm ribbon. Give each a French Knot center using two strands of old gold thread. Surround the flowers with French Knots in four strands of pale willow green thread.

⑰ Work the small remaining area at the left of the design in French Knots using four strands each of old gold and pale willow green thread, and white 4mm ribbon.

Bella Rosa

YOU WILL NEED

Fabric

	Backing fabric (calico or other)
	Pale pink silk 4 x 6 in. (10 x 15cm)
	Pale apricot silk organza 3½ x 5½ in. (9 x 14cm)
	Small piece of ivory lace

Needles

Crewel needle, size 8
Chenille needles, sizes 18, 20, and 22
Beading needle

Embroidery thread

	Thick pale apricot silk
	Thick green silk
	Green
	Apricot
	Antique ivory

Silk ribbon

	Pale apricot 4mm
	Antique ivory 4mm
	Antique rose 4mm
	Green 4mm
	Antique rose 7mm
	Pale apricot 7mm
	Antique ivory 7mm
	Musk rose 7mm

Sundries

4 mother-of-pearl buttons
Small pink beads
9 pearl sequins
Sewing thread

Appliqué, Couching, and freestyle and ribbon embroidery techniques have all been employed here to create this timeless and elegant design reminiscent of the Victorian era.

continued on next page

Bella Rosa
continued from previous page

PATTERN GUIDE

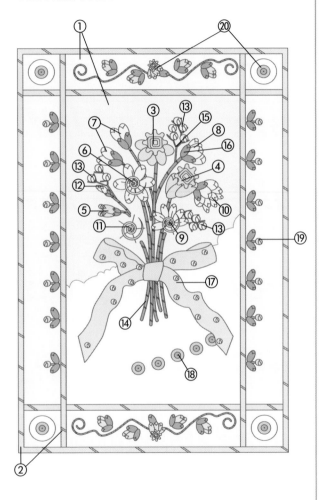

ORDER OF WORK

Prepare fabric

① Place the pale pink silk rectangle on the backing fabric, making sure the grains are running in the same direction. Mark and, using sewing thread, machine stitch a 5½ x 4 in. (14 x 10cm) rectangle in the center of the silk, using very short stitches. Trim away the excess.

Place the pale apricot silk organza in the center of this rectangle. Mark and machine stitch a rectangle 4⅓ x 2¾ in. (11 x 7cm) into position, again using very short stitches. Trim away the excess. You should now have a silk organza center with a silk border.

Place the ivory lace within the bottom half of the silk organza rectangle and machine stitch in place along the sides and the bottom following the silk organza stitch line.

Reinforce the stitching with another machine stitch line right beside the original lines through all layers of fabric.

Stretch the fabric on a hoop. Transfer the pattern to the fabric.

Outline

② Disguise the machine-stitched lines by Couching thick, pale apricot silk thread over them. Use one strand of apricot embroidery

KEY TO STITCHES USED

 Couching, *page 85*

▬▬ Straight Stitch, *page 58*

 Running Stitch & Colonial Knot, *page 73*

▬▬ Ribbon Stitch, *page 63*

thread as the couching thread.

Roses

③ Work the five lower petals of this rose using pale apricot 7mm ribbon and Straight Stitch. With the same ribbon, work a Running Stitch & Colonial Knot just above the Straight Stitches.

④ Using the same ribbon, stitch Ribbon Stitches for the upper petals and work another Running Stitch & Colonial Knot scrunched up against the ends of the Ribbon Stitches.

⑤ For this rosebud, work two Ribbon Stitch petals using the same ribbon, but before piercing the ribbon, wrap the ribbon around the needle as for a French Knot.

⑥ Work five or six Ribbon Stitches radiating out from a central point using antique rose 7mm ribbon. Use antique rose 4mm ribbon to work a Spider Web Rose in the center.

⑦ For each of these two rose buds, work two overlapping Ribbon Stitches in antique rose 7mm ribbon.

⑧ Using the same ribbon, stitch this larger bud in two layers of two Ribbon Stitches.

⑨ Work five or six Ribbon Stitches radiating out from a central point using antique ivory 7mm ribbon. Use antique ivory 4mm ribbon to work a Spider Web Rose in the center.

⑩ Work three layers of three Ribbon Stitches, overlapping the stitches and splaying the last layer of stitches out a little.

⑪ Use pale apricot 4mm ribbon to work a Spider Web Rose.

⑫ Work this rosebud by overlapping two Ribbon Stitches in antique ivory 4mm ribbon.

⑬ Work groups of French Knots using antique ivory 4mm ribbon.

Stems

⑭ To form the large rose stems, Couch the thick green silk thread into position. Use one strand of green embroidery thread as the couching thread.

⑮ Use one strand of green embroidery thread and tiny Fly Stitches to cup around the bottom of the ivory French Knots. Extend the tail of the Fly Stitch to form the stems.

⑯ To form calyxes, work small Ribbon Stitches at the base of each of the rosebuds and the bases of roses 8 and 10.

Bow

⑰ Using musk rose 7mm ribbon, tie a bow. Tack the center to the rose stems as shown. Using one strand of antique ivory thread, Couch the bow to the design with a sprinkling of French Knots.

⑱ Below the bow, attach the pearl sequins and small

pink beads. Bring the beading needle up through the fabric, sequin, and bead, and take it back down through the sequin and fabric. Fasten thread at the back.

Borders

⑲ For the side borders, work Straight Stitch stems in one strand of green embroidery thread. Using pale apricot 4mm ribbon, stitch a French Knot at the top of each stem. Work two Ribbon Stitch leaves on either side of each stem in green 4mm ribbon.

⑳ For the borders at top and bottom, stitch the stem tendrils in Stem Stitch using one strand of green embroidery thread. Stitch the rosebuds in Ribbon Stitch and pale apricot 4mm ribbon. Work the leaves on either side of each bud and one beneath the central rose in Ribbon Stitch using green 4mm ribbon. Work the central roses in pale apricot 4mm ribbon and a Running Stitch & Colonial Knot.

In each corner, bring the beading needle and thread up through the fabric and through a mother-of-pearl button, a sequin, and a small pink bead. Take the needle and thread back down through the sequin, button, and fabric. Repeat this twice more so that three small pink beads finally sit on top of the sequin and button.

 French Knot, *page 70*

Spider Web Rose, *page 112*

Stem Stitch, *page 94*

 Fly Stitch, *page 62*

Glossary

Aida fabric An evenly woven fabric with regularly spaced holes, forming a grid of squares, used for counted thread and ribbon embroidery.

Appliqué The decoration of fabric by attaching shapes cut from other fabrics. Appliqué shapes may be glued or stitched onto base fabric.

Awl A sharp, fine, pointed tool used to create holes in fabric, canvas, and leather.

Batting Natural or synthetic wadding in sheet form used for quilting or padding a design.

Bias binding Narrow strips of fabric cut on the bias (i.e. at 45 degrees to the straight grain) and therefore stretchable, pressed with folds for easy application, used to finish raw fabric edges. Also used to cover a hoop to prevent fabric from marking and slipping when stitched.

Calyx The outer, non-reproductive parts of a flower, composed of free or joined sepals.

Couching Attaching a thread, cord, or ribbon to the fabric surface by stitching it down with another thread.

Evenweave fabric A fabric woven with the same number of threads per inch (2.5cm) in each direction, used for counted, freestyle, and ribbon embroidery.

Freestyle embroidery Any embroidery worked by following design lines rather than by counting threads.

Fusible bonding A web of nonwoven fibers, usually backed with paper, which may be melted with an iron to attach fabric to fabric. Often used in appliqué techniques.

Hardanger fabric A woven fabric made from pairs of intersecting threads in counts of 22 or 24 squares per inch (2.5cm). Used in counted thread, openwork, and ribbon embroidery. The weave of the fabric allows threads to be easily pulled to create patterns.

Interfacing May be a nonwoven or woven fabric that is fused or stitched to the back of fabric to stabilize it and prevent the fabric from distorting in use or during stitching.

Light box A box containing an electric or battery-powered light. The top of the box is covered with a clear sheet of plastic or glass. The light reflects through the glass illuminating a design that has been drawn on paper or fine card or plastic sheets. It is used for transferring patterns.

Linen A natural fiber, woven fabric available in a variety of different weights and textures.

Muslin A very lightweight, woven cotton fabric.

Pure silk A natural fiber, woven fabric with a lustrous finish available in various weights. The weight for silk is termed "mummy."

Quilting Stitching together two layers of fabric with a layer of batting between them.

Satin ribbon May be made from either synthetic or silk fibers. The ribbons may be double-sided, matte, or shiny. Because of the special weave used to produce them, they can have a satin finish on one side and a textured finish on the other. They are usually inexpensive and are available in a variety of different widths.

Sheer ribbons Usually made from spark organdy or georgette. They are transparent and may be printed, embroidered, or plain.

Silk dupioni A textured and lustrous, natural fiber fabric with a fine weave.

Silk organza A finely woven, transparent, natural fiber fabric.

Soluble fabric A plastic-like, transparent material that may be stitched on or used to cover an underlying fabric. The fabric dissolves when immersed in water. It is often used to stabilize fabric or to transfer designs to embroidery fabric.

Shadow work A type of freestyle embroidery worked on the wrong side of translucent fabric, to show as a muted shadow on the right side.

Stabilizer fabric A (usually nonwoven) material used to back embroidery during stitching, to prevent distortion.

Stamen One of the male sex organs on a flower, usually consisting of anther and filament.

Tacking Temporary stitching, usually similar to Running Stitch, used to hold fabrics in place until work is complete.

Textured ribbon Often has a pile such as velvet and is used to create luster and complexity to a design.

Topiary The art of clipping shrubs (such as box or yew) into ornamental shapes.

Vein A strand of vascular tissue in a leaf or other flat organ.

Wash-away pen A fiber-tipped pen filled with either blue or pink ink that dissolves when it makes contact with water. Used for temporary markings on fabric.

Designers and Suppliers

Robyn Alexander

Bella Rosa, page 247

Colour Streams
5 Palm Ave
Mullumbimby
NSW 2482
Australia
Tel/Fax: +61 (0)2 6684 2577
Email:
info@colourstreams.com.au
Website:
www.colourstreams.com.au

Daphne J. Ashby

Flower Border, page 206
Swag of Ribbon Flowers,
page 218
Flower Triangle, page 228
Flower Garland, page 232
Hearts and Flowers, page 236
Ribbon Bouquet, page 238
Country Garden, page 244

Eaton Rise
Eaton-by-Tarporley Lane
Cheshire CW6 9AF
United Kingdom
Tel: +44 (0)1 829 732734

Lorraine Asko

Roses and Cupids Garland,
page 200
Butterflies of Australia,
page 204
Iceland Poppies, page 210

Lojé Embroidery Designs
5 Thaxted Place
Swan View
WA 6056
Australia
Tel: +61 (0)8 9294 2292
Email:
lorraine.asko@bigpond.com

Marilyn Becker

Silk and Organza Daisies,
page 142
Poppies, page 156
Climbing Flowers, page 162
Barcelona Mosaic, page 212

Ribbon Designs
PO Box 382
Edgware
Middlesex HA8 7XQ
United Kingdom
Tel: + 44 (0)20 8958 4966
Email:
info@ribbondesigns.co.uk

Jenny Bennett

Lavender Time, page 234
Lilac in Springtime, page 240

Jennifer Bee
Shop 2, Dove Court
306 Raymond Street
Sale
Victoria 3850
Australia
Tel: +61 (0)3 5143 2899
Fax: +61 (0)3 5143 3129
Email:
jenniferbee@bigpond.com
Website:
www.jenniferbee.com.au

Lee Castle

Chrysanthemum, page 226
Spider Chrysanthemum,
page 230
Pom Pom Chrysanthemum,
page 242

16 Kidman Street
Robina
Queensland 4226
Australia

Pam Cousins

Beaded Holiday Wreath, page 150

Poinsettias, page 154

Rose Bouquet, page 166

Cornflowers, page 170

Dragonfly, page 174

Borders, page 178–181

Alphabet, pages 184–197

Rose Bowl, page 202

Grape Arbor, page 208

Strawberry Delight, page 214

Summer Day, page 220

Weeping Willow Garden, page 222

Victorian Tree, page 224

Angels N Stitches

1744 Feedham Avenue

Kelowna

BC V1P 1L3

Canada

Tel: +1 250 765 2566

Email: prcousins@shaw.ca

Joan Gordon

Say It with Flowers, page 160

Twirled Rose Keepsake, page 164

Seashell, page 168

Celebration, page 176

Magical Garden, page 182

Lewins Lodge

Crockham Hill

Edenbridge

Kent TN8 6RB

United Kingdom

Email: joan@irvinegordon.co.uk

Carolien Jones

Balloons, page 138

Closed Iris, page 140

Flowering Barrow, page 144

4 Heather Close

Farnham

Guildford

Surrey GU9 8SD

United Kingdom

Tel: +44 (0)1252 713353

Email: jonescarolien@hotmail.com

Laraine Lord

Field Daisies, page 172

Gathered Rose, page 198

Twig Heart, page 216

Laraine's On Capri

Shop 25, Commercial Centre

Isle of Capri

Queensland 4217

Australia

Tel: + 61 (0)7 5531 6621

Email: larainelord@austarnet.com.au

Lesley Tarrant

Naïve Lily Pond, page 146

Holiday Wreath, page 148

Sunflower, page 152

1a Wickham Avenue

Shirley

Croydon CR0 8TZ

United Kingdom

Tel: +44 (0)20 8656 3160

Carole Wade

Rainbow Daisies, page 158

50 Chalkpit Lane

Oxted

Surrey RH8 0NE

United Kingdom

Tel: +44 (0)1883 713867

Email: carolethehaven50@ntlworld.com

Index

Acknowledgments

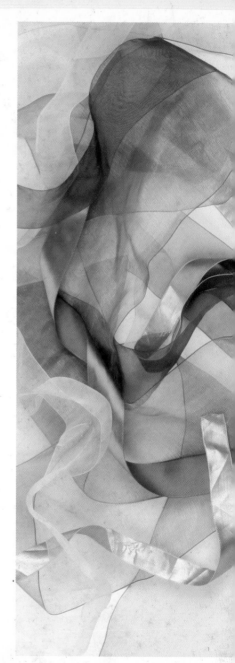

In writing this book, I have had the privilege of working with many creative and highly talented people. I would like to extend a very warm thank you to the Quarto team, in particular Kate Kirby and Jo Fisher, for their support and advice throughout this project. Producing this book has been a team effort. A very special thank you to the artists who contributed the original embroidery motifs and patterns seen in the Motif Library. It is only through their generous spirit and willingness to share their skills that the reader of this book may enjoy and experience the joy and beauty of ribbon embroidery. Finally, thank you to my husband Andrew, my father Bill, and my sister Mary. Your encouragement, humor, and patience kept me focused.

While every effort has been made to credit contributors, Quarto would like to apologize should there have been any omissions or errors—and would be pleased to make the appropriate correction for future editions of the book.